PRAISE FOR *WHY SPIRITUAL CAPITAL MATTERS*

"This book is for those who have seen through the mirage of socially-conscious capitalism and self-aware individualism and their promises to change the world for the better, and are wrestling with the complexities of real work and connection in real communities. Mattson's insightful reflections grow out of highly varied stories of leaders using 'spiritual capital' to tend to whole communities and whole persons, and point the way toward work and economics less captive to the greed and isolation of late-capitalism."

—JON BERBAUM, president, Highland, and cofounder, Design & Innovation Roundtable

"*Why Spiritual Capital Matters*, and the community work Mattson has done to research and present this important topic, is a meaningful contribution to our understanding of what being in business can be today. . . . Craig shines a light on what makes it possible, sustainable, and inspiring to do good work in the world."

—COREY N. M. KOHN, CEO, cofounder, and member-owner of Dojo4, and cofounder of Antidote to Tech

"You know in your gut as a leader that there is more to organizational effectiveness than just strategy and resources. There is an unseen, intangible, but nonetheless essential, third element that is the heart and soul of our work—in short, it's our spirit. Craig's research will affirm your experience and remind you that true organizational success comes from tapping into the power of spirituality in our communities to accomplish our mission."

—LAURA ZUMDAHL, president and CEO, New Moms

"This book is a must-read: It illustrates the power of unveiling how living out your faith in the world opens your eyes to once invisible communities of abundance."

—DEAMON HARGES, faculty member of the Asset Based Community Development Institute and chair of the Grassroots Grantmakers Association Board

"Craig's perspective on business and spirituality is so refreshing, especially for those of us who have been in the 'conscious business' sector for many years. He helps us see with new eyes—ourselves, each other, our paths, our connections. I can't recommend his book highly enough."

—EMILY LONIGRO, founder and president, LimeRed

"Craig Mattson has created a vital resource for organizational leaders everywhere. In our time of widespread spiritual longing, he provides clear and practical pathways to activate the spiritual capital that is always in our midst—and which could not matter more!"

—ANGIE THURSTON, cofounder, Sacred Design Lab

"Equipped with a compassionate heart and professorial pen, Craig Mattson is perhaps the perfect emissary."

—TYLER ETTERS, vice president of Highland

"Craig Mattson's exploration of the essential but invisible element of spiritual capital as it expresses itself on the neighborhood level, by the people making a place where people can thrive in the places they live while fighting to create a just economy, is a weekly listening habit worth creating. It's a viewpoint, expressed in each story from a person creating a neighborhood economics of interdependence that you will enjoy, will inspire you, and will teach you things you didn't know you needed to learn."

—KEVIN JONES, cofounder of SOCAP

Why Spiritual Capital Matters

Why Spiritual Capital Matters

Activating Latent Resources in Your
Organizational Community

CRAIG E. MATTSON

WIPF & STOCK · Eugene, Oregon

WHY SPIRITUAL CAPITAL MATTERS
Activating Latent Resources in Your Organizational Community

Wipf & Stock
An Imprint of Wipf and Stock Publishers
199 W. 8th Ave., Suite 3
Eugene, OR 97401

www.wipfandstock.com

PAPERBACK ISBN: 978-1-7252-6442-7
HARDCOVER ISBN: 978-1-7252-6443-4
EBOOK ISBN: 978-1-7252-6444-1

04/28/21

. . . that which is to be, already is.
Ecclesiastes 3:15 NRSV

Contents

Preface

The Conscious Company Leaders Forum in Santa Cruz may be the most wondrously woo-woo gathering of business leaders in the world. Think of the gifts on offer. Lushly narrated mindfulness exercises. Raw presentations of leaderly epiphanies. Luminous conversations in the redwood chapel. Organic gourmet meals. An impressive amulet-to-person ratio. It's the sort of gathering where people wear loafers so they can, at a moment's notice, put bare soles on the ground and breathe deeply from their diaphragms. Walking out of the hall one evening after dinner, just behind a trio of fairly conventional-looking businessmen, I overheard one make matter-of-fact reference to a recent out-of-body experience. None of this would be customary in my usual conference fare. Academic gatherings don't have prayer pillows or energy crystals, and audience members do not, as a rule, weep during presentations of researching findings. When they do tear up, it is not, to put the matter gently, for reasons of spiritual awakening.

But as my research notebook filled up with nonplussed scribbling, one moment stood out as *the* challenge to all this warmhearted spirituality. I remember a deft moderator concluding a conversation with a seemingly unrelated question. He simply and briefly asked, "What do you need?" There was a silence. And then the mic passed from hand to hand down the row, and each panelist responded with the same, single word. They varied their inflections, their shrugs, their smiles. But they all uttered the same exact thing.

Capital. Capital. Capital. Capital. Capital.

What kicks organizational leaders sleepless in the lonely hours of the night is not an angelic epiphany or mystical vision, but the question of where to get resources, how to access investments, how to get in front of clients, so that the organization can do its work in the world. This book's research has led me into conversation after conversation with company presidents

kept discrete from organizational operations.[1] In a similar vein, sometimes I got the sense from the organizational leaders I spoke with that practicing spirituality feels a little like knowing how to figure-skate. It matters so much on the ice, all that litheness, all that swiftness. But then, once you leave the rink, who really can tell that you know how to skate? Sure, you're perceptibly fit and graceful as you make your way to the conference room for the next personnel meeting. But when you have 154 emails to respond to before the day is out, what difference does it make that you can do a double Axel?

To complicate matters further, organizational spirituality raises perennially tricky questions:

- Isn't it all rightly considered a personal matter? How can managers encourage shared spiritual practice without infringing on the privacy and freedom of employees? Won't it become a site for power abuse?

- Isn't spirituality a matter of inward wellbeing? How can it be shared, except maybe in a let's-all-observe-a-moment-of-silence sort of way?

- Won't spirituality at work contaminate spirit with monetary concerns?

- Isn't spirituality a stalking horse for religiosity? If you integrate spirituality into your organization and make it shareable for a community, and if you draw on specific rituals and practices, won't you inevitably open the door to institutional religiosity in otherwise secular spaces?

Private vs. public. Inward vs. outward. Inspirational vs. practical. Sacred vs. secular. These are confusing oppositions.

Obviously, I'm writing this book because I don't think that economic capital and social capital are sufficient for the wealth and wellbeing of your organization and its community. But before we can develop a concept of spiritual capital and before we can discuss its implications for dealing with overwhelm, conducting critical conversations, motivating the team, and engaging your organizational neighborhood, we should take some time to investigate this love-hate relationship with spirituality in organizational life.

I've spent quite a lot of the last decade researching the interaction of economic and social capital in what you might call the business-activist space. Studying the discourses of cause-related marketing, corporate social responsibility, and social entrepreneurship have confronted me with a widely

---

1. Beaumont, *How to Lead When You Don't Know Where You're Going*, vii, 49–64. Leaders, she insists, should pay close attention to the soul of their organizations and let that awareness guide their efforts at collective discernment. Her counsels for organizational inwardness, I think, draw a different picture than this book's discussion of external economic circulations. Her argument is more focused on inwardness than on what might be called organizational and neighborly "among-ness."

taken-for-granted notion about spirituality in relation to organizational life in late-modern capitalism. Often, my interviewees have spoken as if companies and organizations needed spirituality in order to be more compassionate, holistic, and equitable. But I have come to think that the influence has more often flowed the other way. Instead of spirituality reshaping how we understand our economic and social projects, our socio-economic projects have shaped how we understand spirituality. Of course, corporate and entrepreneurial projects have not been the only shapers of contemporary spirituality: a persistent strain of bad Platonism in the Western tradition, the decline of organized religiosity, and the rise of the social justice mainstream have also profoundly shaped how we understand spirituality today.[2] At the same time, it is impossible to talk about any of these spirituality-shaping forces without simultaneously talking about the ubiquitous mystique of global capitalism.[3] In any case, the highly individualized and interiorized vision for spirituality shaped by capitalism in conspiracy with these other forces has, ironically, proven to be economically impractical. Let me talk about just two windows that my research has thrown open on the ways that socio-economic projects have shaped our dreams for spirituality, instead of the other way around.

CORPORATE SPIRITUAL RESPONSIBILITY

What she wanted to know, this student with her hand raised in a tiny rhetoric class in the winter of 2007, was *had any of us had heard of Product (RED)?* The other four of us shook our heads. "It's pretty great," she said. "You buy RED-branded products, and they give money to fight AIDS in Africa." We looked up the project, and sure enough, somehow Bono and Bobby Shriver's cause-marketing campaign was persuading corporations, governments, charities, and businesses to partner for the sake of resolving the global AIDS epidemic, especially in sub-Saharan countries like Botswana and Angola. A little more research turned up a (RED) Manifesto, featured on a full-page *New York Times* advertisement.[4] I didn't tell the students this at the time, but I was pretty thoroughly baffled by the way the campaign's rhetoric blended

2. My own tracing of spirituality's development through the Western tradition via the decline of organized faith, the spread of globalist capitalism, and the rise of social justice culture relies on Taylor, *A Secular Age,* 505–13; Wuthnow, *After Heaven*; and Burton, *Strange Rites.*

3. For discussion of the "misenchantment" of capitalism today, see especially the prologue to McCarraher, *Enchantments of Mammon,* 1–18.

4. You can see a copy of the (RED) Manifesto here: "The (RED) Manifesto," Internet Archive. See another image of the Manifesto at "The (RED) Manifesto," Modernista!

SPIRITUAL ENTREPRENEURSHIP

One irony in the RED campaign was that its mystic promise was grounded in the communion of mainstream institutions—federal governments, philanthropic foundations, transnational corporations. And from where we sit today, that communion looks hard to believe in, given all the institutional failures in response to climate change and racial upheaval and the novel coronavirus. But even back then, not everybody was buying the notion that big institutional collaborations would save us all. In 2006, the same year that Bono launched RED, a much smaller approach to world-betterment hit the mainstream with the launch of Blake Mycoskie's social enterprise known simply as TOMS. Actually, social entrepreneurs had been around since at least Muhammad Yunus launched his micro-lending Grameen Bank in the early 1970s. But when Mycoskie launched the TOMS company out of his apartment closet, promising to give away a pair of loafers for every pair purchased, social enterprise became a thing faster than you could say *alpargatas*. Social entrepreneurs had Bono's same uncanny optimism, just not for mainstream institutions. The world's problems could be solved, yes, but not by governmental or philanthropic approaches.

My interviewees have made disappointment in mainstream institutions explicit. Maiken Piil, a social entrepreneur in Copenhagen told it to me bluntly: "We can't wait for the political system and the politicians to catch up with reality."[12] Andy Swindler, another socially mindful business consultant, agreed: "Government resources are gone."[13] What about the big philanthropic foundations? Surely, we need Bill and Melinda Gates? Kendra Foley agreed that the world still needed philanthropy. But she was also running the social enterprise Make Work at the School of the Art Institute in Chicago, and from that vantage point, "the nonprofit model needs some serious attention." Too often, she noted, it confuses "having a big party" with "getting at the root of the cause."[14] Robert White, who helps to run the social enterprise Cleanslate at Cara, puts the matter more starkly: "Charities are over. Dead. Finished. Instead of a strategy that relies on asking and giving, from here on in, we're going to be earning our way. Contributions, once seen as donations, are increasingly being replaced by investments with an expected rate of social return."[15]

12. Piil, interview by author, April 3, 2019.
13. Swindler, interview by author, February 15, 2019.
14. Foley, interview by author, February 13, 2019.
15. White, "From Giving to Investing."

As I listened to social entrepreneurs talking about social problem-solving, I heard the same script over and over again: *mainstream institutions have failed; social innovators need to step up, use shrewd business aspirations, and solve some wicked problems!*

What I didn't see coming as I started in on a book about socially entrepreneurial communication—tossing a RED-branded Starbucks cup and buying some TOMS loafers instead—was that this emergent sector had inaugurated a new vision for personal and organizational spirituality shaped powerfully by the socio-economic norms and structures in late-modern capitalism. The fragmentations and accelerations of globalist economics and digitally mediated society had given these company presidents and sectoral leaders an intense dream for uniting company operations and family life and social work and personal wellness into a single way of being. Kendra called it the One Life Approach.

My first encounter with this approach came while watching Mycoskie perform his smiley American alternative to Bono's ironic Irishman. Mycoskie told his twee Texas conversion story this way: he was suffering burnout from all his entrepreneurial projects and so had taken a trip to Argentina to play polo and drink red wine. (Not a spiritual recovery plan available to most entrepreneurs I've spoken with, but that's another story.) One afternoon, he fell in among social workers who persuaded him to help them deliver shoes to needy orphans. Mycoskie had such a good time doing all these good deeds that he decided to launch a company that would make that sort of generosity profitable—er, sustainable. I once heard Mycoskie telling a conference audience that the injunction in the book of Proverbs to give of your first fruits provided biblical rationale for his buy-one-give-one model.[16] But whatever the theological grounding, Mycoskie's company made gift language central to their messaging. Their website and advertisements and even their packaging would be saturate with the language of gift. Instead of year-end reports, they've offered Giving Reports. They would call their new products "gives." For a while, Mycoskie would even call himself TOMS's Chief Giving Officer. Mycoskie said he didn't see why he had to spend the first half of his life making money and the second half giving it away. He wanted one life in which making and giving were parts of a seamless whole.[17]

He was only among the first of the social entrepreneurs I heard speaking this way. Tim Brand told me how he "left the corporate world . . . because I just felt like I was splintering as a person, and I didn't like that in myself." He hated the thought that at work his life went one way, and at home his family went

---

16. "Blake Mycoskie," YouTube video.
17. "Changing the World," *CNN*.

another, and at church the congregation went still another way. He wanted a holistic life, so he started a social entrepreneurship called Many Hands for Haiti.[18] Corey Kohn was helping to run a successful software company when she and her colleagues got sick of the pointlessness of the work. They started over with a social enterprise called DOJO4. Today, Corey says, she takes great joy that she leads "a company where people feel happily engaged in their work, where they feel like their work is useful, where they can hopefully somewhat easily support their families and that the work supports the things that make them happy in their lives." She calls that provision of a holistic life, "the most important part of our mission."[19] Let me cite one more example: Sarah Woolsey had long thought that too many things in her life and church had "seemed very siloed." Her diagnosis was that "here you have business and work, and then over here we have church, and over here I have philanthropy, and then maybe volunteerism and family and then friends." So, when her church agreed to lease a building to her for a dollar a year for a decade, she started the Impact Guild, an incubator, which she describes as "this massive experiment to bring those things into a lot more integration with one another and not feel like they have to be parsed out like so much." The difference has been all the difference even for her family: "So my husband and I moved to two blocks from the Impact Guild . . . because it felt very important. And with that we've made choices to walk to the nearby restaurants and the nearby coffee shops and go down and spend time in the community garden."[20]

I started filling composition notebooks and Evernotes and Google drive folders with epiphanies and revelations and aspirations from social entrepreneurs from London to Colorado, from Texas to Chicago. I taped posters of qualitative research codes to my office wall—concepts like "resourcing the spiritual" and "manifesting karma" and "apophatic accounts of reality." I transcribed interviews about mindfulness and generosity and inspiration and insight until I was tired of typing—and then found money to hire out still more transcriptions. I went to conferences called Conscious Company Leaders Forum or SOCAP, focused on intersections between finance, business, entrepreneurship, and values. Their stories were funny and earnest, joyous and fearless by turns.

And then came 2020 and another intercontinental virus. This one required no cause-related marketing campaign to catch my attention.

Like so many others for whom the novel coronavirus became unignorable in the spring of that year, I fell out of organizational life into the

---

18. Brand, interview by author, February 18, 2019.

19. Kohn, interview by author, May 10, 2019.

20. Woolsey, interview by author, March 27, 2019.

dispiriting quietness of shelter-in-place. Instead of driving to work each morning, I lay in bed in the morning, listening to all the traffic *not* happening. And then, taking up my phone as the coffee brewed, I eyed pandemic numbers that belied all wellbeing. The Trump administration's steady erosion of mainstream institutions—the dismissals of public health, the financialization of the economy, and the tribalization of legislative bodies—made a teetery American society look imminently collapsible.[21] It was an uncanny time. The direst of social problems, a novel coronavirus, was not just over there somewhere in Africa, located well and far away from day-to-day operations, but was instead in the aerosols of everyday organizational life. The large-scale institutions upon which Bono had grounded his business model for world betterment proved incapable to keep at bay the death of 500,000 Americans from COVID-19, easily the most angering result of institutional breakdown especially at the federal level.[22] The killings of Ahmaud Arberry, Breonna Taylor, and George Floyd resulted in a widespread sense that institutions were not just failing but actually designed to exclude huge swaths of the citizenry. To complicate matters further, even the heroic social entrepreneurs with their holistic lives were beginning to look uncannily optimistic—especially from the perspective of a Black Lives Matter protest.

UNCANNY AND CRUEL OPTIMISM

Corporate social responsibility and social entrepreneurship had given new life to an ancient and modern dream of spirituality in which everything that holds together does so thanks to the inner life of powerful individuals.[23] In our own time, business activists were making plausible two claims, that attention capital saved lives and that personal wholeness can bring together what globalism has put asunder. The resultant spirituality has, at times, seemed reassuringly competent. What Richard Lanham has called Attention Economics implies that the capability to think about thinking, to shift focus to focus itself, makes society malleable.[24] Our big problems, being of our own making, can be unmade with a change of heart and mind. But 2020's racial upheaval, rioting, protests, White defensiveness, and pandemic have all put in question the societal efficacy of inwardly focused spirituality,

21. Packer, "The President Is Winning."

22. Healy, et al. "The weapon that will end the war."

23. The next chapter will discuss a significant voice in my own narrative account of how so much of modern life has come to rely upon inwardness and subjectivity: Crary, *Suspensions of Perception.*

24. Lanham, *The Economics of Attention.*

ence in socially entrepreneurial spaces suggests that the economic and the social don't go together as easily as many of my White research subjects would like to think.

The entrepreneurs of color I've spoken to are very far from giving up on using their economic and social capital to improve the wellbeing of their program participants and organizational communities. Allen told me in our third interview, with no small a sense of satisfaction, that Cincinnati had gone from being a sort of entrepreneurial desert to being a destination for Black-owned entrepreneurship. He felt sure that Mortar's part in that was significant.[37] But working within the structures of conventional business and global capitalism as Black organizational leaders has meant cultivating a different kind of spiritual capital than my research had as yet uncovered.

One of the first interview subjects I reached back out to after sinking down into shelter in place was DeAmon Harges, a self-described social banker from Indianapolis. DeAmon talked about economics in a way I found initially bewildering. He spoke of moving millions of dollars in his neighborhood in some of the not-so-prosperous sections of Indianapolis. *What is he talking about?* I wondered. He would also tell of going to neighborhood homes and asking folks to tell him a story. He would catalyze these stories with a simple prompt, something like, *Tell me the story of how you were born.* Or *Tell me a time when you gave money away without expecting anything in return.* The questions he asked people, he said, would "pull you and the rest of your ecology into it."[38] In this way, he said, he was able to bank neighborhood narratives about gifts that were circulating in his community.[39] The resources he was pointing to were both economic and social, but they were hidden until his storytelling and story-listening activated them, pushing them into neighborhood circulation. I wasn't sure I'd heard anything like this among all the people I'd interviewed.

The longer that I've mulled over what DeAmon said, the more I've learned that what he's roving for is a resourcefulness that doesn't superimpose uncanny optimism on state or corporate programs (though he makes use of both), nor does it tax the inner lives of powerfully innovative individuals (though he strikes me as one of those). Instead, the knack that DeAmon alerted me to and exemplified in his practice has everything to do with making visible resources that are already present in his neighborhood. His goal is not to rescue others or to lift others up. His goal is to recognize hidden vitality, to spot inconspicuous liveliness, to attend to the barely perceptible

---

37. Mattson, "You Are Not Your Start Up—Allen Woods."
38. Harges, interview by author, April 13, 2020.
39. Harges, interview by author, April 13, 2020.

happenings of a community's ecology. I'll have more to say about DeAmon in a later chapter. But suffice it to say for now that meeting him helped shift my attention from an impractical dream of spiritual inwardness to an organizationally competent construal of spiritual capital. After I met him, I started indexing this resourcefulness everywhere. I'm writing this book in hopes that you'll take up a similar accounting.

PLAN FOR THE BOOK

By now you have it clearly in hand that this book is not a woo-woo guide for infusing your organization with good vibes. Nor is it a manual for inspirational organizational practices. Instead, the empirical research and conceptual exploration of this book focus on the need for leaders to catalyze economic potential in their organizations and neighborhoods. This is not a book about why you should become a social entrepreneur. But social entrepreneurships are, I have found, good machines to think with, to borrow a phrase of I. A. Richards, because they constantly see their organizations as neighborhoods within neighborhoods.[40]

The next chapter narrates how spiritual capital differentiates from other kinds of capital. What makes it spiritual, I argue, is not just that it enacts a certain kind of awareness, but that it *participates* in an encompassing economy, which might be life-giving or soul-killing. Either way, that participation activates economic and social capital as mutually involved domains of life, not separate concerns that somehow need tying together with the help of big institutions, nor held united in your heart and mind. Spiritual capital can, in fact, shift social hopes from the allegedly vast potentials of the human spirit, which recent experience has shown is all too exhaustible, and instead attends towards farther horizons in what Wendell Berry has called the Great Economy.

Chapter 2 attends closely to a central problematic of organizational spirituality today: *how do leaders pursue organizational effectiveness and organizational wellness simultaneously?* How, in other words, can workplace community be a site for productivity without becoming at the same time a site for burnout? Whereas the maxims of health and wellness discourse often center on personal accumulations of spiritual insight and awareness, the urgent orations of wisdom literature (especially in the Old Testament book of Proverbs) direct us to how such insight and awareness might circulate in community. A focus on personal spiritual accumulation can *sometimes* mediate organizational strategy and organizational wellness, but my research

40. Richards, *Principles of Literary Criticism*, vii.

suggests that often enough the processes of accumulation are not the same as the equally vital processes of circulation in productive organizations. This chapter centers, in short, on the economic and social possibilities that individual mindfulness can all too easily miss.

Chapter 3 discusses dialogue as a beloved approach to circulating wellness in an organization. Although spirituality in organizations often gets envisioned in terms of some kind of conversation—with oneself, with another, and with Being itself—careful reading of the book of Job suggests what dialogue too often disguises. After examining the shortcomings of this conversational approach to organizational spirituality, I close the chapter with practical recommendations for moving towards multilogue rather than dialogue. Chapter 4 turns to another mode of circulating wellness throughout an organization: inspirational storytelling. But instead of the heroics of inspirational narratives, my research data, along with the book of Ecclesiastes, commends a fresh mode of narrative, the Neighborhood Story, subsequently discussed in Chapter 5. The final discussion in Chapter 6 takes up what has become the gold standard of meaningful work—organizational impact—and asks what spiritual capital might have to do with that pursuit. Instead of impact, I propose that expanding the range of our shareable feelings is one important way that social entrepreneurs are helping their communities participate in the Great Economy.

The central critique underwriting this book centers on a misguided daydream about spirituality's role in organizational projects. We are right to long for an integral role for spirituality in our organizational communities, but we have misconstrued that role far too often. It is simply not the case that mainstream economics has bracketed the personal and the meaningful from its calculus; to the contrary, the worlds of business management and organizational life are suffused with sentiments and significances. Unfortunately, these literatures and discourses and practices do not locate the often-hidden resourcefulness of workplace communities and the subtle sufficiencies of our nearby neighborhoods. My hope is that reflecting on the stories that this book relates, will suggest to you a fresh pattern of organizational engagement, one in which spiritual practice brings overlooked resources into practical and profitable networks of wellbeing.

1

Spirituality and Capital in Organizational Life

You know when you're sitting on a chair and you lean back so you're just on two legs and you lean too far so you almost fall over but at the last second you catch yourself? I feel like that all the time.

STEVEN WRIGHT

ORGANIZATIONAL LEADERSHIP IN THE best of times requires a knack for teeter. Developing strategy, doing research, curating social media, measuring program effectiveness, balancing the books—none of these tasks tilts a company in just one direction; each asks for fast and frequent micro-adjustments, like the chair-tilting of the comedian. Administrators have always had to make pivots regarding services provided or curtailed, staff kept on or let go, branding expanded or re-expressed. But in the last few years, as the gig economy in a rapidly evolving information society has accelerated to unnerving speeds, as the political climate has gone uncanny, and as pandemic has settled in, my research among organizational leaders suggests that running a workplace has come to entail more soul-care than ever before.

Some of this pastoral imperative arises from trauma endured by Black and Brown staff members in everyday American life. As mainstream institutions have proven unable to provide justice for all, organizational leaders have felt obligated to compensate spiritually somehow. But administrative work with people in every demographic has come to entail spiritual care, especially as people seek transcendent meaning in their work. Derek Thompson has called this occupational phenomenon "workism," or the belief in "a kind of religion, promising identity, transcendence, and community" in the workplace.[1] The research that led to this book has pulled me into conversation after conversation with company presidents, program directors, business managers, and nonprofit practitioners—whose tasks increasingly seem to require more than the teeter of the chair-tipping comedian above. Given all that has gone so unjustly wrong, so socially and economically off-kilter, leadership some days seems to entail something closer to levitation than teetering. One common approach to this set of challenges entails securing one's own spiritual wellbeing as a way to care for the souls of others.

BRINGING THE SOUL TO WORK

Martin Rutte was having a bad time and for no good reason. His professional life was thriving. His marriage was in great shape. He was enjoying good health. And yet he was in a deep funk, so deep in fact that, despite his Jewish faith, he found himself in the back row of an Augustinian monastery during Mass, staring dull-eyed at the ritual proceeding up front. And then, abruptly, he found himself weeping and not quite whispering the phrase, *It's about God.* He went back to work with those words still on his mind and started suggesting to co-workers that maybe spirituality should have a place in the world of business. His colleagues got wide-eyed and anxious: "'No! No, no, no, are you crazy! No, no, no, you'll lose your reputation. People will think you're proselytizing. Don't do it, don't do it, don't do it.' And everybody said that. Everybody."[2] But Martin wouldn't give up. First of all, he pointed out, Jews don't convert anybody to anything. But, secondly, he said, there's nothing to convert people *to.* Spirituality is not an answer, but a question—an ongoing question, he added. It's the questioning itself.

Today, Martin runs a consultancy business that inspires organizations and their leaders to slip out of it-just-has-to-be-this-way thinking and into why-can't-it-be-another-way sort of thinking. You can read stories about

---

1. Thompson, "Workism Is Making Americans Miserable."
2. Rutte, interview by author, May 3, 2019.

this approach to professional life in *Chicken Soup for the Soul at Work*.[3] Or you can seek out the conversations that Martin regularly holds with people, asking them what his most recent book, *Project Heaven on Earth*, calls "the three questions that will help you change the world . . . easily." During the course of our interview, he turned the tables on the conventional researcher/subject relation and asked me these questions:

1. Recall a time when you experienced Heaven on Earth. What was happening?

2. Imagine you have a magic wand and with it you can create Heaven on Earth. What is Heaven on Earth for you?

3. What simple, easy, concrete step(s) will you take in the next 24 hours to make Heaven on Earth real?[4]

His questions took me to blue-skied memories from childhood and compelled me to think about some of my own epiphanic moments. And all the while, Martin smiled at me mischievously like a twenty-first-century Socrates twinkling at an unwitting Athenian.

I love Martin's story, and I admire what he's done since the 1980s to advocate for workplace spirituality and to quicken discussions of work as a place to seek personal meaning. Even if you haven't read Martin's blog posts and books or attended conference presentations, you have read trade books and listened to podcasts on wellness at work, all of which purvey something like what he has helped to make commonsensical in organizational life. Aaron Brice of Ambient Inks named this commonsense in relation to his own employees:

> [B]usiness owners are focused on the wrong things . . . so spirituality is a way to look at that with fresh eyes and be like, okay holy s––t, I am actually, there is actually some wisdom here that I'm maybe avoiding. In terms of day-to-day stuff, the more in tune I am with what I need on a deeper level, the more I can help bring that out of people, the more patient and better listener I can be for other people.[5]

The taken-for-granted work of spirituality, in other words, is how to move mindfulness from my soul, so to speak, to yours. As a result, administrators tend to focus on the person-by-person accumulation and transfer of spiritual insight, often by holding brave conversations or by telling inspirational stories.

3. Canfield, et al., *Chicken Soup for the Soul at Work*.

4. Rutte, *Project Heaven on Earth*.

5. Brice, interview by author, April 10, 2019.

But in my research among organizational leaders and consultants, the moves that turn this spirituality into capital do not come easily. Maiken Piil told a story about a friend of hers who had practiced contemplation for many years, a woman who knew how to slip gracefully into a profound inner silence. But at work, Maiken noted, this meditative practice proved to be of little consequence.[6] Andy Swindler told me that in meditative practice, it's possible to "[c]ollect a lot of really beautiful, often poetic information about purpose," but he finds that he has to help his clients "actually bring it back to the world of ego," by which he means something like the self-interested world of economic practicality. An epiphanic insight is great, even essential. "But," he says, "it's not really actionable."[7] In turn, the CEO who's been coached by someone like Maiken and Andy has to go to work and duplicate that consultancy through yet more brave conversation and storytelling. Because most people's training in business school did not include a section on pastoral care, this well-intentioned work runs quickly into obstacles. Tim Kelley, a business consultant on spiritual matters, told me that sometimes when organizational leaders have an epiphany like Martin's, they say, "I found my purpose. It was really cool. You all should too. So now we're all going to go find our purpose."[8] But if the administrator doesn't provide what Tim calls "business justification," then confusion results. The manager says, "I meditate. Meditation is good. You should all meditate"—and the team member says, "And why the f–ck am I doing this?"[9] Tim worries that spiritual interventions can actually foster "a real and sometimes panicked sense of lack of safety, because I don't know what the boss is going to ask me to do next that has nothing to do with my job."[10]

Tim's comments point to another concern. Even if business leaders manage, by dint of dialogue and inspirational storytelling, to bridge the gap between spiritual insight and economic practicality, how can these leaders avoid an inappropriately profit-driven intrusion on people's inner lives?

This attention to the worker's inner life may have made managers more considerate, more therapeutically savvy, but it has also made them more skilled in the cultivation of what Malcolm Harris has called "human capital," or the leveraging of people's capacities for the sake of corporate profitability.[11] Because organizational spiritual practice can enable employees to work

6. Piil, interview by author, April 3, 2019.

7. Swindler, interview by author, February 15, 2019.

8. Kelley, interview by author, April 19, 2019.

9. Kelley, interview by author, April 19, 2019.

10. Kelley, interview by author, April 19, 2019.

11. Harris, *Kids These Days.*

longer hours, write more reports, and sell more products, it is all too easy for managers to charge business expenses to the slush fund of employee inner peace. And this isn't a conundrum for organizational leaders alone. The employee almost certainly wants to bring her whole self to work. But she just as surely doesn't want the boss to own her whole self at work.

Urging attention to inwardness and subjectivity in organizational life and leadership is nothing new. Historians like Jonathan Crary and Nikolas Rose argue that, throughout the twentieth century—and, really, even as far back as the mid-to-late nineteenth century—business administrators have sought to intervene on the inner life of workers. For Crary, this focus on the subjective experience of employees arose in tandem with late-1800s' "imperatives of attentiveness" for people to be more "productive and orderly, whether as student, worker, or consumer."[12] In the twentieth century, as Rose tells the story, this attentiveness to professional subjectivity contributed to the formation of what one of his chapters calls "The Contented Worker": "Productivity, efficiency and contentment were now to be understood in terms of the attitudes of the workers to their work, their feelings of control over their pace of work and environment, their sense of cohesion within their small working group, their beliefs about the concern and understanding that the bosses had for their individual worth and their personal problems."[13] These histories relate how managers have made their employees' attentiveness, motivation, and moral improvement (however that be defined) integral to the successful organizational project.

David Miller has traced the development of "Faith at Work" social movements, quoting a business school professor as saying, "There were two things I thought I'd never see in my life, the fall of the Russian empire and God being spoken about at business school."[14] But the spread of religious and spiritual discourse is hardly surprising given the massive disruptions of vocational and organizational life described by economic historian and theorist Nigel Thrift: "The three shocks which have produced the current situation are . . . political, technological, and theoretical."[15] The first of these has to do with "the increasing stress on subjectivity, and the politics of recognition that accompanies it." As capitalism has become more reflexive, more self-regarding, Thrift points out, a therapeutic expertise has come to seem essential to every aspect of organizational life.[16] Managers commonly

12. Crary, *Suspensions of Perception*, 22–23.

13. Rose, *Governing the Soul*, 70.

14. Miller, *God at Work*, 105

15. Thrift, *Knowing Capitalism*, 20.

16. Thrift, *Knowing Capitalism*.

While writing this book (and trying to fathom the mind of God), I spent a fair amount of time reading the essays of a Kentucky farmer named Wendell Berry. He wasn't a likely candidate, I'll admit, for understanding organizational communication or economic theory. And he doesn't conceptualize spiritual capital, so far as I can tell. But he is nonetheless invaluable when it comes to construing how organizations participate in larger orders of things. I remember one morning, holding my hurriedly brewed coffee in one hand and, in the other, a carefully written piece called "An Argument for Diversity," in which Berry argues for distributing productivity broadly and variously in agricultural community. It was not an essay about prayer or meditation or yoga; it wasn't even about the suburban information economies where most of my interviewees do their work. But the piece gave me a cue to spiritual capital. "Obviously," Berry said in a way that was only barely obvious to me at the time, "we need to stop thinking about the economic functions of individuals for a while, and try to learn to think of the economic functions of communities and households."[24]

I took a long draw of coffee and decided to take his advice. Instead of asking about how to accumulate lots and lots of inner peace as spiritual capital, I started asking about how working community might learn to recognize the hidden gifts already and diversely present in their midst and in their neighborhoods. Gradually, over the course of many mornings with Berry and bad coffee, a counterintuitive hunch started to take shape. Being spiritual at work might not mean holding space for deeper consciousness in the sacred now, or whatever. What it might mean instead is learning to recognize with others the latent and diffuse resourcefulness of a workplace community. I developed, through a painstaking process of conceptual testing with interview subjects and practitioners in the social entrepreneurship field, a concept of spiritual capital as *the capability to recognize and catalyze a community's hidden possibilities for participation in an encompassing economy.*

What makes this definition *spiritual* is, firstly, that it involves recognizably spiritual practices such as awareness and discernment and, secondly, that it participates in a larger order of things. The spirituality of this capital is not, in other words, its intangibility or invisibility, but rather its immersive involvement in some encompassing, usually overwhelming, order. This order of things may be entirely material and humanly derived, as in the enormous systems of global capitalism. That sounds counter-intuitive: what's more soul-killing than the mainstream economy? How could saving big money at Menards be *spiritual*? As Eugene McCarraher has argued, though,

---

24. Berry, "An Argument for Diversity," 539.

participation in global capitalism is not necessarily soulless and unspiritual. It is redolent with mysticism and enchantment, even when dehumanizing and environmentally destructive practices make it "mis-enchanting."[25] But when we treat global capitalism as all-encompassing, we get uncanny capitalism. It's spiritual, all right, and even, in a sense, religious. But as an encompassing order, or a pseudo-Great Economy, global capitalism fails to comprehend all that is.

A comprehensive order may include the intangible and the invisible, as in the case of participation in what Wendell Berry calls the Great Economy, which he defines theologically as "the ultimate condition of our experience and the practical questions rising from our experience." Berry locates the greatness of this economy in the way it includes quite simply everything and everyone. "We are in it whether we know it or not and whether we wish to be or not."[26] He locates the economics of the Great Economy in its inclusion of "principles and patterns by which values or powers or necessities are parceled out and exchanged."[27] This overwhelming order of things invites participation much as the Tao does in Eastern thought, or Being does in continental philosophy, or the reign of God does in Christian teaching. Human organizations are little economies, Berry would say, that either cooperate with that Great Economy to their benefit or against it to their harm.

When Somali refugees in Minneapolis fund real estate purchases, not by purchasing a conventional mortgage—a practice that would transgress their Muslim convictions against usury—but through small-scale neighborhood philanthropy, they are deploying spiritual capital. When Kevin Jones helped these Somalians to achieve this, not by solving all their problems in their stead, but rather by helping to *release* their capabilities to provide for their own community members, he was practicing with them a kind of discernment that proved to be spiritual capital. He didn't say, "Look folks, here's how things work in the U.S. banking system. Let's just get you a mortgage under my name." Instead, he asked them how things worked in what they saw as God's economy and worked with that.[28] Jones and the Somali-Americans are making economic decisions, in other words, as if the ultimate horizon for their action is not the American banking system, but rather an overwhelming revelation of a way that humans should be and act.

---

25. McCarraher, *The Enchantments of Mammon*, 11.

26. Berry, *What Matters*, 116.

27. Berry, *What Matters*, 118.

28. Nonko, "Minneapolis' Somali-American Community."

SPIRITUAL CAPITAL CONTRASTED

No doubt, you've been thinking about other kinds of capital conceptualized within the past half a century so. We have the neo-Marxist sociologist Pierre Bourdieu to thank for conceptualizing forms of capital alternative to economic assets. He defined *economic capital* as those resources that are "immediately and directly convertible into money and [that] may be institutionalized in the forms of property rights." He defined *social capital* as those resources that come in the form of connections with and accountability to other people. But he most famously delineated *cultural capital* in three ways: all that accompanies personal formation and embodied inculturation (e.g., physical fitness and speakerly capabilities), cultural artifacts (e.g., artworks and book collections), and institutional certifications (e.g., diplomas and accreditation).[29]

A quick example should illustrate Bourdieu's concept of cultural capital. As a college professor of communication arts, I spend most of my time helping my students as organizational leaders of tomorrow accrue sufficient competence to speak appropriately, to write clearly, to comport professionally, and to complete an accredited undergraduate college degree. All that is cultural capital. But it has what you might call a dark side: cultural capital is a constant site for power and struggle. As a result, cultural assets make us feel, as Kenneth Burke would say, *"goaded by a spirit of hierarchy"* and, worse, *"rotten with perfection."*[30] Even when it comes to spiritual capital, Bourdieu would see it as another form of the human's ceaseless lurching towards status. He would not, however, acknowledge that some forms of spiritual capital entail participation in a transcendent order of things—something like Wendell Berry's Great Economy.

But most of my interviewees, when they hear about spiritual capital, think first of Robert Putnam's more benevolent notion of *social capital*, which he defines as "social networks and the associated norms of reciprocity."[31] The story he tells is of "a powerful tide [that] bore Americans into ever deeper engagement in the life of their communities" until because of late-modern cultural forces, "that tide reversed and we were overtaken by a treacherous rip current" with the result that "we have been pulled apart from one another and from our communities."[32] Noting that our community groups either "bond" us tribally or "bridge" us generously, Putnam takes on the

29. Bourdieu, "The Forms of Capital."
30. Burke, "Definition of Man," 16.
31. Putnam, *Bowling Alone*, 21.
32. Putnam, *Bowling Alone*, 27.

native individualism of American society and critiques our tendency to isolate ourselves from others, "bowling alone" when we might do democracy together.[33] To the degree that spiritual capital involves us in communities of one sort or another, Putnam's concept partially overlaps with the concept this book will be developing, except that spiritual capital in these pages is more often a way of recognizing hidden forms of social capital—that is, social networks that have not yet been animated for the good of the organization or its neighborhood.

More recently, Chris Rabb has combined Bourdieu and Putnam to frame what he calls *invisible capital*, or "the toolkit of our skills, knowledge, language, networks, and experiences, along with the set of assets we were born with: our race and gender, our family's wealth and status, the type of community in which we were raised, and the education we had as children."[34] As an African American entrepreneur, Rabb is fully acquainted with the unfair distributions of information and knowledge capital in contemporary society. But he doesn't stop with Bourdieu-styled critique. He goes on to Putnamize entrepreneurship by debunking the individualist mythology that individual hard work and genius will make any startup succeed. Instead, he insists that entrepreneurs need to accumulate the often-unspoken knowledge that actually makes for flourishing companies and communities. Bowling alone is unlikely to contribute to democratic thriving; businessing alone is just as unlikely to succeed entrepreneurially. Although his concept sounds a good deal like spiritual capital—it's invisible, after all!—he doesn't distinguish between the hidden capital of one's skills and networks and the spiritual capital needed to uncover that capital. He doesn't mention, for instance, the spiritual challenge entailed by discerning what's invisible in a person or a community. He tends to assume that invisible capital is easily recognizable once his book names it. But the process of activating subtle or latent or dormant economic and social capital is essentially mysterious because these resources participate in an even larger order of things than the mainstream economy in which his entrepreneurial hopes largely rest.

When it comes to *spiritual capital*, popular authors like Danah Zohar and Ian Marshall have urged organizational leaders to cultivate an inner resourcefulness that infuses values and meaning in economic life. "Spiritual capital," they argue "is not monetary wealth" though it creates "the possibility of making a profit—perhaps even more profit—by doing business in a wider context of meaning and value."[35] This sort of asset is not social capital,

---

33. Putnam, *Bowling Alone*, 22.

34. Rabb, *Invisible Capital*, 6.

35. Zohar and Marshall, *Spiritual Capital*, 21.

trying to practice."[41] He told me he wasn't particularly religious, though he'd shifted from atheism to agnosticism. "Recently, I've been like, I don't know. It's been an ongoing change."[42] I took another look at my list of spiritual practices and, on a hunch, asked him if my list looked like it was designed by a White guy. He said that the thought had occurred to him—but "only because meditation isn't something that's practiced by people of color. It also plays into mental health, which is another thing people of color is bad at addressing . . . In our culture, it's not something that's practiced. Mental health is something that's . . . bringing more awareness into people of color households. It's on the right path to getting there, but it's not there yet."[43] I scribbled some more notes in my notebook and thought about my next question.

Then, Devonta interrupted with a query of his own: "How does race play into entrepreneurs coming here?"[44] I looked up from my notebook, a little discomfited. He added, "I always feel like 1871 wasn't for black and Brown people."[45] As it turns out, some research does suggest—I looked it up later—that incubators like 1871 aren't always great for minority entrepreneurs, at least not as much as for their White "bro" counterparts. Worse, incubators can extract people from their communities out of an "expectation that those who live farther than a reasonable driving distance will move away from home for the duration of the program, which is often several months," an expectation detrimental to lower-income people of color (and to women) with household or neighborhood obligations.[46] Sure, Devonta conceded, places like 1871 try to be inclusive—especially by giving out scholarships for their programming—but "I'm pretty sure nobody in the neighborhood knows what this thing is."[47]

We agreed to meet for a follow-up interview in that neighborhood, on 63rd Street, the main boulevard of Chicago Lawn, where Devonta had lived most of his twenty-four years of life. Because we were in the thick of COVID-19 at the time, we met on the main boulevard of Chicago Lawn. We found two separate park benches, six feet apart, with an H6 recorder between us, each of us holding a microphone, like we were about to burst into song together. Instead, we were staring across the street at the property

41. Boston, interview by author, February 14, 2020.
42. Boston, interview by author, February 14, 2020.
43. Boston, interview by author, February 14, 2020.
44. Boston, interview by author, February 14, 2020.
45. Boston, interview by author, February 14, 2020.
46. "Creating Inclusive High-Tech Incubators," JPMorgan Chase & Co.
47. Boston, interview by author, February 14, 2020.

he hopes one day to buy—or, as he's more likely to put it, to buy back. And as we talked, he kept his eyes on the street, reading the signs, noting the happenings. Buses roared by, and delivery trucks, filling out our conversation with smoggy ambient sound. Listening to the recording again, I can hear someone trudging across the street, dragging a trash bin.

I think, because my questions at 1871 had been so individually focused, it took a while for it to register just how important Devonta's neighborhood was to his formation. I suspect that I was listening for the Martin-Rutte-styled epiphanic story, the story of spiritual awakenings. Devonta can tell that kind of story when he wants to. He told me about his high school English teacher who prodded him to think long-term about what he was going to do with his life. He told how other people kept telling him to get a college degree or join ROTC—and how no one mentioned the possibility of entrepreneurship. Or he talked about the time that he and his friend were glum-scrolling through Twitter, lamenting how the only sustainable Black fashion brands were White-owned, until one of them said, in effect, "Let's just start our own brand." But most of the time, it seems to me, Devonta's stories were too diversely interactive to fit neatly into the paradigm of spiritual awakening. They were stories about paint-and-sip gatherings, open-mic nights, brand showcases, and a real estate venture called "Reclaiming the Hood."

Devonta's stories weren't trying to transfer a capsule of inspiration from his inner life to mine. It was more about conveying to me a mode of attentiveness. He describes himself as a "real big observer, just seeing how things work."[48] As we talked, I got the sense of someone beholding 63rd Street in a way that I couldn't quite manage yet. I use that spiritually inflected language, *beholding*, because it approaches a richer, more participatory way of seeing. He looks at those storefronts and sees the past and the present together, a once prosperous street teeming with economic life and now an economically depressed region. When I listen to him talk, I hear a yearning for residents to be out and in the streets and under the trees, eating together, playing together, owning their lives together. The stories he really loves to tell are those about what his neighborhood once knew how to do and could learn to do again.

> I found out that my community used to have a holiday parade for 26 years and they stopped in 2009. [I ask him, "A holiday parade?"] Yeah, it used to be in November, December. It just stopped out of nowhere. And I was thinking about how 63rd Street used to be the highest economic strip next to downtown, back in the day, and I was like, everything that my community

48. Mattson, "Reclaiming the Hood—Devonta Boston."

had that was positive was taken away. And I was like, we should just bring back the parade.[49]

We should just bring back the parade. That's the kind of community action that Devonta wants to circulate, wants to see lived out in his own organization and in his neighborhood. But the parade is a parable in another sense as well. Think about it: a carnival procession brings out into the open the economic and social goods of a neighborhood, making them joinable, shareable, danceable. Until the parade comes along, it can be easy not to see the resources of a neighborhood. The boarded-up strip malls that look in ruins. The furniture tossed in the dumpster. The green space that's overgrown with weeds. All that may be inconspicuous economic capital, awaiting someone like Devonta to see it with the right kind of beholding. But besides those economic resources, there are also inconspicuous human networks. The teens circled up on the basketball court. The people that run the corner food-and-liquor. The congregation that meets in the storefront. All that is social capital, and it, too, may go unnoticed—until the parade comes back. Along comes a Devonta, or a whole neighborhood of people with visions like his, and suddenly that economic and social capital rounds the corner and comes into view.

This book is an attempt to describe the spirituality essential not only to discerning hidden economic and social capital, but also for moving it into circulation in workplace communities and their neighborhoods.

THE SPIRITUAL AND THE CAPITAL

Nigel Thrift notes that capitalism today has become exceptionally *knowing*, in the sense that we say, "She's a very knowing person" or "That was a knowing remark." Capitalism has become that kind of knowing, that kind of self-aware. It talks about itself and to itself endlessly in journals and conferences and blogs and trade books and TED Talks and online journals.[50] But the quest for spiritual capital suggests that most modes of capitalism do not know or comprehend nearly enough. As Berry says, "the thing that troubles us about the industrial economy is exactly that it is not comprehensive enough, that, moreover, it tends to destroy what it does not comprehend."[51] Berry notes that such capitalism is profoundly impractical, which is a peculiar thing to say about a highly utilitarian complex like the world of business

49. Mattson, "Reclaiming the Hood—Devonta Boston."
50. Thrift, *Knowing Capitalism.*
51. Berry, "The Two Economies," 116.

exchange. But Berry notes a terrifying impracticality to all the waste and misuse of natural and human resources. I'd like to append to his critique of industrial capitalism my own observation that the attentional and affective capitalisms of our information society are similarly impractical. They do what they do by *not* comprehending how awareness actually functions in an organization, how generosity actually moves in a neighborhood, how love actually circulates in community.

When Berry points economic action towards a more comprehending order, he refers to the largest and most knowing economy conceivable, calling it the Great Economy, "known and unknown, visible and invisible, comprehensible and mysterious."[52] As a Christian, he construes the Great Economy as quite simply everything that exists under the reign of God, although I suppose that many of my interviewees, holding to different religious or irreligious standpoints, might think of this as simply the big household of the world in which we dwell together. Whatever we call it, though, Berry warns us against the perennial temptation of treating our organizational projects *as* the Great Economy itself. It is only as we recognize the rules of this mysterious household—rules about squandering and sustainability, for example—that our capital functions as it should, not as delusional energy but as renewable resource.

In other words, it might not be a scarcity of spirituality that creates the conundrums of workplace life today, but a surplus of spirituality vaguely understood. The result of this vagueness, I fear, is economic impracticality in the workplace communities in which we pour out our very selves. As Berry laments, many of our approaches to capital today are excessive and therefore profoundly impractical. When it comes to economic capital, for example, how long exactly do we imagine this earth can sustain all the clear-cutting, strip-mining, and fracking needed to keep our plastic consumables in circulation? I think a similar superfluity happens with our expenditures of attention and affect. We often produce messaging at a rate that suggests that human awareness is somehow an infinite resource. We often tell heroic but sentimental stories as if inspiration were a similarly inexhaustible good. We often pursue organizational impact at a rate that suggests the jump from quantitative to qualitative change will inevitably happen if we can just find the right metric and *push*. To borrow a term from Berry, many of our endeavors are actually "anti-economic" moves, because they offer no stay on human desire, no recognition of neighborly potential, no mutuality of relation.[53]

52. Berry, "The Two Economies," 118.
53. Berry, "The Two Economies."

academic inquiry in the experiences of businesspersons, especially women and people of color.

Although you will see me alluding to critical theory, my deepest reading focused on the wisdom literature of the Old Testament, especially the books of Job, Proverbs, and Ecclesiastes. I have listened to these wisdom voices, often uncomprehendingly, all my life. But in the course of this project in particular, I found them indispensable to understand what Ecclesiastes calls the "unhappy business that God has given to human beings to be busy with."[56] The three sages at the heart of these books—Job, Lady Wisdom, and Qoheleth—are fiercely unsentimental. They despise vagueness. Like many of my interviewees, these sages speak from places of spiritual loneliness, often with impatience and even contempt for the dogmatism of the traditions that had so powerfully shaped them. Job's bewilderment at the obliviousness of his pious friends reminded me of my research subjects frustrated by organized religion. Qoheleth's puncturing of the religious commonsense of his day and Lady Wisdom's urgent indignation reminded me of how my interviewees inveighed against churchly abuses and happy-clappiness about truly wicked problems.

But what was even more important than anything these sages had to say was the way their enfolding stories configured them in community. Job, Lady Wisdom, and Qoheleth, after all, are literary characters, and learning their wisdom entails learning the stories that enfolded them. The protagonists always draw our attention, but it is easy to miss the way that these protagonists are not entirely reliable—except in relationship to their encompassing story. If you just take notes on everything Qoheleth says, for example, you'll find yourself tangled in all his contradictory insights. If you read Job, as I have for most of my life, as a purveyor of insights, you'll miss the fact that at the end of the book he puts his hand over his mouth and stops talking. It's what the proverbist is doing with the figure of Lady Wisdom, it's what the writer of Job is doing with his hero, it's what the editor of Ecclesiastes is doing with the sage Qoheleth that most helped me to look for economic circulations within organizational neighborhoods in keeping with the vast circulations of the Great Economy.

---

56. Ecclesiastes 1:13 NRSV.

2

On Being Mindful and Overwhelmed

Nothing in the course of my research interviews so irked my interlocutors as cheap talk about mindfulness. One interviewee reported hearing at a conference on business-focused spirituality about a goal to "scale mindfulness." She spat out, "What the f–ck is that?"[1] Another interviewee burst out, in the middle of one of my questions, with a complaint about over-priced spiritual retreats to locales like Hawaii. My interviewee laughed angrily: "Like, f–ck you. I don't want to rage, but don't tell me that that's what I need to do to have a more balanced life."[2] Another person worried about people being *forced* to be mindful at work. He described a hypothetical manager who says, "I meditate. Meditation is good. You should all meditate"—and then imagined a team member responding, "And why the f–ck am I doing this?"[3] Still another interviewee reversed that scenario with a story about disagreeing with her employees' pietism. She looked at me in indignant amusement: "You may hear this, and go, 'What the hell is she talking about?'" She described herself as being "in the tumble dryer of it."[4]

Conversations about spirituality don't usually evoke this sort of intense language. But these exchanges did, sometimes in tones of sarcasm or even anger. The affect registers, I think, an angsty question at the center of

1. Hinton, interview by author, March 31, 2019.
2. Kohn, interview by author, May 10, 2019
3. Kelley, interview by author, April 19, 2019.
4. Knowles, interview by author, April 17, 2019.

attentional practice in organizational life today: how to understand the role of mindfulness in the tensioned work of pursuing organizational mission and cultivating organizational wellness. On the one hand, many interviewees celebrated attention as a lavish good. Meditative practice and plentiful self-care should provide the business administrator all the awareness needed for life and leadership. As Tiff Hinton said,

> I feel like when I'm kind of aligned fully to my spirit and to my purpose, there's an overflowing of joy and abundance and love. And when I have that, I naturally want to give it and I naturally want to. But it's a cycle. The way that I can expand in my life is by giving of my love, joy, and abundance, right? So, if that's overflowing out of me like a river, I want to share that with others because that way it creates more space within myself that I can expand and grow and continue to evolve and learn. And so, for me, I feel like when people are practicing spiritual things that are real and aligned, truly aligned, they should be in a place of love and joy and abundance. And so, I feel that naturally starts to overflow.[5]

When organizational leaders like Tiff spoke of awareness, they tended to use this language of spontaneity, abundance, and flow. For them, the central maxim would be something like, *Awareness is ample; give it freely.*

On the other hand, business leaders feel compelled to negotiate attention as if it were a scarcity that obliges careful, disciplined, rational distribution. Accordingly, the organizational administrators I spoke with in the course of this research had often given a great deal of thought to how public awareness might be focused, how a trainee might be informed, how a brand might be designed to cut through a cacophonous mediascape.[6] They had, in other words, absorbed the wisdom of contemporary self-help literature often entitled with arresting one-word headers: *Distracted*; *Quiet*; *Rapt*; *Focus*; and so on.[7] The core maxim of these books on attention economics is as follows:

> When it comes right down to it, there is no such thing as free attention; it all has to come from somewhere. And every time we place an additional demand on our attentional resources—be it

---

5. Hinton, interview by author, March 31, 2019.

6. I did speak with Kate Jakubas, a detergent manufacturer, and with Adam Melnyk, who was involved in electronics recycling. But apart from these two exceptions, most of my research subjects ran organizations that trafficked in information and attention.

7. Jackson, *Distracted*; Cain, *Quiet*; Gallagher, *Rapt*; Goleman, *Focus*.

by listening to music while walking, checking our email while working, or following five media streams at once—we limit the awareness that surrounds any one aspect and our ability to deal with it in an engaged, mindful, and productive manner.[8]

As my interviewees built this sort of thinking into their business models and organizational missions, they could be quite distrustful of mindfulness discourse. For them, the guiding maxim was something along the lines of, *Attention is sparse; spend it wisely.*

I learned from both these attention economies.[9] But what catches my ear in the indignant obscenity of some of these same interviewees, especially in response to cheap mindfulness talk or social obliviousness, reminded me of similar outbursts in the wisdom literature of the Old Testament. If you've ever thumbed through the book of Proverbs, you know it's full of practical maxims like, "A slack hand causes poverty, / but the hand of the diligent makes rich."[10] But in the middle of all these balanced couplets bursts a larger-than-life figure, Lady Wisdom, who strides straight out of a rabbi's fervid imagination and into the crowded streets of ancient Israel, where people are busy doing business and talking politics. I suppose I usually imagine Wisdom to look like Plato in his robes or maybe like the robeless *Thinker* of Rodin's sculpture. But here, Wisdom is a woman who stands, shouting, crying, calling to distracted passersby at intersections so chaotic that only a shouter could be heard. "How long, O simple ones, will you love being simple?" Or as one of my interviewees expostulated, "What the actual f is going on here?"[11] Wisdom's cry, says theologian David Ford, is "a sign of the limits of speech, a gesture towards the inadequacy of any words to this content, an indication of the superlative, of breaking the bounds of terms and categories, of transcendence."[12] It's a cry that resounds throughout scripture, says Ford, and throughout the world. I thought I detected its tones even in a leader's indignantly transgressive word choice.

---

8. Konnikova, *Mastermind*, 73.

9. The concept of an attention economy I have drawn from Lanham's *The Economics of Attention.*

10. Proverbs 10:4 NRSV.

11. Lonigro and Cardona-Maguigad, interview by author, January 25, 2019.

12. Ford, *Christian Wisdom*, 19. Two thinkers have shaped my understanding of overwhelm as a mode of spiritual capital. The first is David Ford, especially in his book *The Shape of Living*, 17–25. The second is Martin Laird, whose discussion of depression and other intractable problems has suggested to me the unexpected resourcefulness of holding a space for what is neither desirable nor essentially resolvable. See especially *An Ocean of Light*, 185–94.

with Asmina or Laura, when I can tell that they're kind of like, oh my gosh . . . They don't have to tell me, "I'm freaking out over this project." Part of my job here is to be . . . observant of that and be able to, kind of like, anticipate these things and give guidance . . .[16]

Maiken Piil, a social entrepreneur in Copenhagen, insisted in our conversations that personal spiritual awareness itself can bring business profitability. For her, contemplative practice is more than an approach to personal wellbeing. For example, she had a client whom she said was "really, really, really good at meditating," but who could not direct it towards business impact. Maiken explains, "she never actually transformed anything or grew. She was just good at meditating, but she couldn't apply that knowledge to the rest. She couldn't apply that practice to the rest of her life." Maiken began working with the woman, teaching her how to accumulate a contemplativeness that would make a difference in the world—and then things began to change.[17] Experiences like this encourage Maiken to honor "the transformational and creative power that is available to us when we partner our spiritual nature with deep consciousness."[18]

As I listened to people like Tiff, Julianna, Jeff, and Maiken reflect on possibilities for melding strategic focus and personal mindfulness, I thought I could discern a useful script in their recommendations for personal soul-care: *Whatever else I cannot manage about the external world, at least this, in here, I can control. I can manage what narratives I allow to cycle in my head; I can control my attitude and determine my intentions. I can decide how mindful I will be. I can select the object of my attention.*

This script, as it happens, enjoys currency in the broader attention economy. Even a power-obsessed TV show like *Billions*, for example, portrays professionals dealing with fragmented lives through their immense powers of concentration. More than one character on the show uses a smartphone app to meditate, among them a hedge-fund titan: "To be Bobby Axelrod is to keep so much in your head, just to keep it from blowing up your brain takes Benedictine-monk-like discipline."[19] Little wonder that scriptwriters are infusing meditation into their plots when, as Tara Isabella Burton notes,

Concepts like 'mindfulness'—a secularized version of principles associated with Zen Buddhism—have become ubiquitous in our

16. Lonigro and Cardona-Maguigad, interview by author, January 25, 2019.

17. Piil, interview by author, April 3, 2019.

18. Piil, "Meet Maiken."

19. Kim, *Billions*, "Short Squeeze."

workplaces, while the onetime meditation practice of yoga—associated with both Hinduism and Buddhism—has now become a $16 billion a year empire in the United States, as much associated with wellness culture and fitness as with spirituality proper.[20]

What shows like *Billions* dramatize, though, is how easily mindfulness can become subservient to the transactionalism of economic exchange.

After talking with my research subjects, it seems clear to me that mindfulness *can* function as a way to unite organizational strategy and economic effectiveness. And for many days out of the year, that arranging of things can work quite well, especially if you're judicious like Emily Lonigro at Lime Red Studio. She speaks with bluntness about the stress and fatigue of running a company while trying to deal with the overwhelm of life as a whole:

> I spiritually had an incredibly hard . . . year and that impacted the business significantly. So just a lot of stuff's been going on . . . I'll be divorced on—a week from today and it's taken all year to get that far. And that was part of that catharsis that from starting in the woods of removing just toxic situations from your life, but it's not like you can decide overnight to just remove that or decide overnight to change the course of your company, which is what we're kind of doing too again.[21]

Faced with confusion and overwhelm, Emily resorts to more intense self-care: "I rein in process, so, like, I'll start meditating again. I'll start working out again."[22] Many professionals like Emily track with a sort of Attention Economics Cycle, in which they spend their concentration to the point of deficit and then have to find more attentional funding. Most, I suppose, experience this deficit as simple tiredness; you go home, go for a run, get some sleep, and, like Emily, you're back at it again. But it is possible for some professionals to fall into a kind of exhausted indebtedness from which recovery is extremely difficult.

The pained and sometimes angry cries of utter exhaustion in contemporary culture are clearly audible for anyone willing to listen. Anne Helen Peterson, for example, has become a voice for this difficulty in describing fatigue not just as a momentary burnout, but as a perpetual state of overwhelmedness: "Why am I burned out? Because I've internalized the idea that I should be working all the time. Why have I internalized that idea? Because

20. Burton, *Strange Rites,* 24.

21. Lonigro, interview by author, June 20, 2017.

22. Lonigro, interview by author, June 20, 2017.

everything and everyone in my life has reinforced it —explicitly and implicitly —since I was young."[23] After describing this exhaustion, Peterson asks, "So what now? Should I meditate more, negotiate for more time off, delegate tasks within my relationship, perform acts of self-care, and institute timers on my social media? How, in other words, can I optimize myself to get those mundane tasks done and theoretically cure my burnout?"[24]

But can we pay attention to this overwhelm, not as something to be "solved" by mindfulness exercises, but as a site for wisdom? Might there not be wisdom, as we practice awareness for awareness itself, in acknowledging that this overwhelm is with us, simply, hugely, bluntly, undeniably? And when it comes to organizational life and leadership, when it comes to dealing with clients and contracts, might there not be a spiritual capital overlooked in the hard-to-deny fact, that sometimes becoming more aware also compels us to deal with what we cannot finesse, what we cannot manage? I heard something of this wisdom in Maiken's storytelling, so let's return to her interview for a moment.

She relates that, during the summer and fall of 2018, she suffered a kind of breakdown that required her to adopt a painful but healing course of action: she stopped working altogether. You know, probably, from your own experience how dispiriting and disorienting it can be to pull away from your daily routines and from the deadlines and obligations that provide momentum through the world. But Maiken was determined not to pretend to be better off than she was. Like Thoreau, she went to the woods. She took long walks, giving time for that awareness of self and the world to gather again. By dint of watchfulness and waiting, she recovered her sense of her own wisdom and resourcefulness. She returned to a place of readiness, found a willingness once again to return to work. She could begin again to offer spiritual wisdom to others.

But when she returned to work, she found herself back in the same burned-out place again six weeks later.

I feel I should emphasize what a resourceful person I personally found Maiken to be. Despite this story, or perhaps because of this story, there were points during our conversation, when I wanted to throw away my role as researcher, toss my notebook, and simply ask for Maiken's help. But where does this resourcefulness come from? What is the ground of her spiritual capital? After mulling over her stories and her counsels, I think a significant part of her helpfulness comes from her willingness to be overwhelmed. She doesn't throw up her hands at life; she doesn't give up on business practicality; and

23. Peterson, "How Millennials Became."
24. Peterson, "How Millennials Became."

she certainly doesn't stop her meditative practice. But she recognizes, some-how, that neither her effectiveness nor her wellness is finally up to how hard she works. This can be on some days a terribly difficult place to be. "I'm sit-ting there with a knot in my stomach, sometimes thinking, 'Am I completely crazy or naive or stupid or, you know . . . f–cking up my life here . . . ? I have to take a deep breath and get back into and just see what actually shows up in my life."[25] Her question felt to me like wisdom's cry.

Maiken's candor here, I think, highlights a core finding of this chapter's discussion: just how precarious, how contingent, how woundable we are as spiritual beings. We live in a world of complex institutional, ideological, and technological forces that pull on the self from every direction. The contest with data-mining algorithms is nowhere near a fair fight, even for the most mindful, the most *aware* person. We are none of us so buffered as we, in our most peaceful moments, imagine ourselves to be.[26] But what can be sur-prisingly resourceful is befriending our own fragility, as Maiken tries to do. Growing accustomed to our overwhelm can itself be a kind of good in that it generates a healing awareness of the precarity of all other selves as well.

AN ECONOMICS OF SCARCE AWARENESS

Some of my interviewees saw organizational strategy and workplace well-ness as more or less irreconcilable concerns. For them, the pursuit of per-sonal spiritual wellness could actually be *distracting* from vital strategies to meet organizational goals. They tended to imply, at least, that organizational attention was a scarce resource: why not spend it on the forceful and pointed concerns of a company's mission? Do your staff members feel fatigued? Do they feel confused? There is strength to be found in reminding everyone what exactly the company was designed to do in the world.

Let's start with a Chicago-based accelerator, 2112. Amor Montes de Oca and her colleagues have spotted a major problem in the entertainment industry—that young innovators and artists struggle to break into the in-dustry—and have responded with a solution, an arts-focused incubator. 2112's operational staff is small, just three people, and running the place sounds highly connective, enormously fun, full of vital encounters—and re-plete with lots and lots of work. When she talks about 2112's work, guiding music recording artists and videographers into the obscure networks that

25. Piil, interview by author, April 3, 2019.

26. And there doesn't seem to be a way to elude these machinations. "People may even stop using Facebook full stop," a *Guardian* journalist concedes, then adding, "But will they stop Googling, watching TV, or sending emails?" Noor, "There are plenty more."

constitute their industry, she focuses on the services that 2112 provides for people who feel bewildered by the work of launching a startup. What Amor didn't talk about much was cultivating organizational wellness within her own staff. She seemed, especially at first, reticent about talking about herself much at all. Mostly, she preferred to talk about facilitating her clients' flourishing: "I've always been behind stage and, just, making opportunities, providing spaces for these things to flourish and bring artists and audience, in a very simplified way, just connecting two entities that should know of each other."[27] She communicated that she and her colleagues work hard, move fast, and practice servant leadership. She told an admiring story about how the president of the company once saw a malfunctioning vacuum cleaner and, instead of asking somebody to fix it, immediately sat down to repair it himself. The picture I got was of an organization whose administrators and staff had given themselves over fully to their shared mission.

Amor did confess that it felt good to talk about organizational spirituality, not just for the sake of 2112's mission, but for the sake of her own wellbeing:

> I guess I really appreciate the opportunity to think back . . . We go so fast and we have so much to do that it's tough to stay reminded of our goals and why we do it and how we go about it. So it's been a great experience to kind of bring it back home and ground it. We go a gazillion miles an hour and we're constantly tired and constantly doing things and stuff. You do it without knowing, without calling it something, and it's nice to have that retrospect. I appreciate it.[28]

Allen Woods runs another incubator, the Cincinnati-based neighborhood accelerator Mortar, and finds the work to be constantly spilling over across all personal boundaries. The strategic work of the organization—to animate and educate entrepreneurs of color towards sustainable business—could easily fill as much of every day as Allen is willing to give. He notes, too, that he cautions entrepreneurs about this, reminding them that they are not their enterprise. They have an identity outside their pursuit of mission, and if they do not cultivate this identity, nourishing their soul through hobbies and sabbath rest, they will not be able to build a sustainable business. He notes that the entrepreneurs of color he works with face a great deal of discouragement from structural injustice, which circulates stories in their head such as, "Nobody's gonna fund me anyway. Or they're gonna tell me to

27. Montes de Oca, interview by author, April 4, 2019.
28. Montes de Oca, interview by author, April 4, 2019.

pull myself up by my bootstraps."[29] Given those obstacles to entrepreneurial mission, they must simply take the time they need for themselves.

For Allen, who has now taken over as the executive director of Mortar, the mission sometimes becomes altogether too much. He pushes back against the pressures of trying to get ahead in a constantly hungry information society where the "hyperalert" worker is slowly devoured by mainstream hurry and rush.[30] But Allen had, just days before our final interview, done the wondrously impractical thing of entering an art contest. His entry wouldn't get him a grant, wouldn't advance his company, wouldn't improve his status or output as an entrepreneurial leader—but would nonetheless feed his spirit. He spoke of "trying to discover who I was before Mortar started, what have I sacrificed to get where I am . . . It's like we're leaving pieces of our selves along this trail, and—it's like, I gotta pick up all my pieces so that I can find all the parts of me that used to bring me joy when work wasn't all that there was."[31] For Allen, the attention required for his work at Mortar and the awareness of soul he needed to recover were in what sounded like a perpetual competition.

Jos Knowles of the socially entrepreneurial nonprofit Beyond the Streets turned out to be another person for whom strategy and mission competed with mindfulness and wellness. She told hard stories about how she and her staff disagreed about whether or not to hire a person of faith for an open position. The organization's U.K. context meant that they could face legal consequences if they discriminated on the basis of faith—unless the position could be shown to require religious commitment. "And it's in a really risky place—that if we make a decision about, yes, that person has to be of faith, we risk the legal side. And if we don't, we risk losing staff. So, where's the spiritual place? Where does spirituality intersect with risk, with growth? That to me is going, oooh, that feels like a very narrow space."[32] Jos was focused on the candidate's abilities; her staff was focused on having a colleague they could pray with in the midst of the work. Jos spoke of the two as creating terrific dissonance for her: "I have no answers, I just have lots of pain around that moment, and I have lots of questions."[33]

Sometimes, my research subjects emphasized mission rather than wellness out of an apparent skepticism for wellness discourse. When Stacey Burns looked at my list of spiritual practices, she smiled deprecatingly at the

29. Mattson, "You Are Not Your Start Up—Allen Woods."

30. Harris, *Kids These Days*.

31. Mattson, "You Are Not Your Start Up—Allen Woods."

32. Knowles, interview by author, April 17, 2019.

33. Knowles, interview by author, April 17, 2019.

heading labeled "Awareness." Mindfulness, she admitted, was "what challenges me the most." I had originally met her at a socially entrepreneurial conference over breakfast of steel-cut oats and blackberries and coffee. After breakfast, we joined other attenders in communal meditative practices, breathing deeply, releasing thoughts. But Stacey found this too much: "I had to excuse myself at one point, because I was like, *I cannot sit in this room with my feet flat on the floor and my eyes closed for another 30 seconds. I have hit my limit.*"[34] The meditative practice essential for her line of work, she felt, had less to do with anything mystical than it did with a knack for bringing one's experiences to bear on puzzling business questions—and, perhaps even more fundamentally, getting informed conversations started in the thick of the business world. That's how you get work done, she conveyed, not through better diaphragmatic breathing.

At the Better Business Bureau of Colorado and the Colorado Institute for Social Impact, Stacey works constantly to help businesses inform their publics about their philanthropic efforts. Companies can be strangely reticent to talk about their altruistic projects.

> I won't make a blanket statement, but I think the folks that have been most resistant to telling their story in that way would offer [as a reason for their reticence] some type of organized religion that they are a part of. Whether they tie those two things together, or it's just that inner sense of how they've been raised or what they believe. The few that I can think of that, really, I mean, millions of dollars that they're putting into this community, but they're hesitant to brag about that because of a religious belief.[35]

For Stacey, pursuing concerted strategy rather than holding onto impractical pietistic convictions is what actually does good in the world. Businesspeople can increase the good they are doing simply by making others aware of possibilities for generosity. Awareness-raising has to do with making essential information available for wise expenditures of attention. This is the kind of attention economics that proves productive in a time when no one has enough awareness to squander.

Serial entrepreneur Cathers Pearson had, in the course of her career, also focused on mission over wellness, out of skepticism for pietistic spirituality in the institutional church.

> I did still have a sense of what I guess you might say, in Christian language, a vision of what the kingdom of God is. What I

34. Burns, interview by author, May 22, 2019.

35. Burns, interview by author, May 22, 2019.

believed how the world should be. And all the injustices and brokenness and lack of hope, all of that—I really wanted to be involved in that work and to see restoration and reconciliation and justice and be a conduit for that. But I was a bit done with the church and I felt like the best way that I could keep tethered to spirituality or to God was by doing. And no longer by going to church or reading the Bible or singing. And all of that seemed so meaningless. But the work felt important.[36]

When our paths crossed, Cathers was beginning to think that perhaps she had foreclosed the spiritual too much. She was, she said, ready to reconsider how spirituality might be of assistance in the work of organizational mission and social justice pursuits. But like Jos, she had faced a difficult question about whether or not she should hire a chaplain. While helping to run the first ethical cleaning company in London, Make Good, one of her investors strongly urged that her team needed a pastor. Cathers shrugged off the advice, pointing to the impact they were missionally committed to, which was providing a good wage for people in service industries. But this donor argued that, no, the spiritual wellbeing of Make Good's employees was also a vital part of their organization's impact. Cathers didn't dismiss the spiritual needs of the team she was managing, but she couldn't see how a chaplaincy was essential to pursuit of their outcomes. "I was wary of the agenda," she said. "I'll leave that there."[37] What mattered, she couldn't help feeling, is spending the time, energy, and attention you have on the organization's mission.

Andy Swindler sat across from me at the Avondale Coffee Club one Friday afternoon and told me about his work running a consultancy agency called Lead from Love. But for all his advice to practice a spirituality of self-care, Andy's experience with a failed business venture makes him rigorously practical. He holds his beliefs about spirituality and people-care with a grin and a shrug. He notes cheerily, "I'm all about Oneness and Unity Theory. I believe we are all energy. I believe everything's connected—all that good stuff."[38] But he nonetheless experiences an unavoidable doubleness in mundane human experience, a doubleness that requires oscillation. By way of analogy, Andy used our positions at a small table in a noisy shop as an illustration of the inevitability of distance and differentiation:

> [W]e exist in this physical reality—or this thing we perceived as
> a . . . physical, dualistic reality where you're there and I'm here.

36. Pearson, interview by author, April 3, 2019.
37. Pearson, interview by author, April 3, 2019.
38. Swindler, interview by author, February 15, 2019.

Unlike both—as long as this is the experience I'm receiving, I'm not going to fight that. There's some reason we're here, right, that we've separated, that we've individuated from Oneness.[39]

He confessed to feeling "slightly shy about using the word *spiritual*," in part because it had not always proven pragmatically necessary in his consultancy, but also because there were times that what he called the "trusted source," a higher being or mode of being from which we can occasionally derive insight, disregards the elementals of human life. He explained, a little wryly, that "the spirit world doesn't always care about basic needs."[40] We may look to our trusted source, whatever that is for us, for "different kinds of wisdom, something beyond human." But a spiritual trusted source, Andy suspects, is not likely to be concerned about physical hungers. The spirit "doesn't always care about money or food, anything, you know," so we can hardly expect compassion or solicitousness from the world of spirit.[41] Andy struck me as a person patient with contradictions, not least because he was on a journey, looking for how spirituality might bridge two pursuits he loved equally well: personal wellness and business effectiveness.

I admire the realism of this scarcity approach to attention economics in organizational life. People like these folks exhibit an industrial strength pragmatism when it comes to focusing on organizational mission. Their insistence that you can focus on this or that, but not both, respects the different modes that mission effectiveness and people-care often require. And given those differences, why not simplify things by keeping the main thing the main thing? But the problem with this sometimes good-natured, sometimes vexed distrust of wellness discourse is that it can overlook the ways that pursuing organizational strategy requires respect for what animates people, what draws people on. The top-down, highly cognitive approach to attention economics exemplified by this get-stuff-done approach to organizational work underestimates the role of desire in human labor.

I learned the importance of taking time for motivating and encouraging others from Kendra Foley, who exemplifies a business leader whose exhausting work has required her to attend to the spiritual dimensions of vocation. In her work as a fundraiser (at the time of our interview, for the School of the Art Institute in Chicago and for her social enterprise Make Work), she struck me as a person with a laser focus on the next action step. But even so, she recognizes limits to checking off the to-do list. She is also someone who has more to do than can ever be put on a list. She allows

39. Swindler, interview by author, February 15, 2019.

40. Swindler, interview by author, February 15, 2019.

41. Swindler, interview by author, February 15, 2019.

this sense of vocational fullness to turn her to personal spiritual practice. "I derive incredible energy from the things that I care about, and if I can always go back to why am I doing this, that usually gives me the energy that I need."[42] This mindfulness helps her keep her team working concertedly. Sometimes, she looks past the mile-long list of things that her team needs to do for a given campaign and instead, addresses the team's exhaustion: "We're going to dedicate the next forty-five minutes to team-building, by personally connecting and reflecting back on what speaks to you the most about the strategic direction of this institution that we're here to support."[43] There are always more things to do than she and her staff have time for. But to ignore the demands of the personal and the spiritual for Kendra is not finally sustainable either. Her experience points, I think, to an easy-to-overlook spiritual good, a kind of awareness-in-the-midst-of-overwhelm that has less to do with achieving personal wellness and more to do with leveraging overwhelm for the good of the world.

The people whose stories and ideas I have discussed have allowed themselves, in a sense, to be productively overwhelmed by the presence of social problems that refuse to go away. Jos focuses on sex trafficking, for example, an economic and sociological predicament that cannot be resolved quickly. Nor does the problem get better if the people in Jos's organization *feel* better. This problem is what contemplative theologian Martin Laird might call an "uninvited guest," an unwanted resident of our late-modern life.[44] Human trafficking hangs around capitalist enterprise's sunny commerciality like someone's tendency towards migraines or depression. It may be that the best that can be done, in the near term, is to keep aware of these uninvited guests, to allow them a presence in our awareness, as Jos and her teammates strive to do. These are problems we would rather not have around, but Jos's complicated affect—good-humored, self-deprecating; fiercely determined, morally indignant—gave her, I think, an ongoing sense of overwhelm, which in turn gave her the gift of a pained but compassionate social awareness.

AWARENESS AS SPIRITUAL CAPITAL

This book offers an extended examination of the limits of inwardness for navigating organizational life and leadership. By looking for the

42. Foley, interview by author, February 13, 2019.

43. Foley, interview by author, February 13, 2019.

44. Laird, *An Ocean of Light*, 185–218. Laird informs this chapter's discussion of how "uninvited guests" expand social awareness.

resourcefulness of a kind of capital that moves among persons rather than simply within them, I am hoping to pull organizational spirituality out into "the among" of the workplace. But of course, spiritual life does have an interior dimension. But instead of seeking a place of unruffled interiority, I have been exploring the potential economic and social importance of an overwhelmed awareness. I have been asking, *what are the goods that come from permitting oneself to be in-the-thick-of-things as an organizational leader?* Let me sum up with a few other ways that spiritual capital makes other kinds of capital visible.

For some of my practitioners, an overwhelmed awareness generates not only spiritual growth but also productive engagement in the world. Richard Tafel is a minister and an entrepreneurial mentor, who, when he looked at my list of suggested spiritual practices, noted: "Awareness is probably the most important one for me, because it precedes all other change. If you're not aware, which most people I think are not, there's no ability for spiritual growth." He noted that some people hope to grow spiritually by retreating to a closeted, pietistic space. He described them as keeping themselves constrained to a sadly all-too-manageable living space." They're living in a bubble or their worldview is very, very small." He conceded that sometimes private retreat is necessary: "I think you do need to be in a space to listen to God or guidance, and that becomes increasingly difficult in a culture that is loud and busy and noisy." But for Richard, there has to be a connection between the quiet spaces of spiritual withdrawal and the robust spaces of everyday engagement. "I, for example, would not be a fan of someone who said, 'I'm going to just develop my spiritual life; I'm leaving behind the world to go pray.' I would say you develop your spirit by engaging in the world and that you are here to be useful and good to others."[45] Richard's observations help to locate a kind of spiritual capital in the overwhelm and busyness and chaos of everyday life that is reminiscent of Dietrich Bonhoeffer's description of his own "this-worldliness":

> living unreservedly in life's duties, problems, successes and failures, experiences and perplexities. In so doing we throw ourselves completely into the arms of God, taking seriously, not our own sufferings, but those of God in the world—watching with Christ in Gethsemane.[46]

Spiritual capital can highlight needed changes in company policy. As a Sufi Muslim with a Master of Divinity degree, Mark Silver runs a

---

45. Tafel, interview by author, May 1, 2019.
46. Bonhoeffer, *Letters & Papers from Prison*, 370.

consultancy called The Heart of Business. He spoke to me in a hushed, gentle voice, making use of ritual gestures, addressing oneness and peace, repeating maxims such as, "We are not separate from source," and "There is no beard in the sky." He is clearly accustomed to the work of helping others to ponder spiritual realities, even from diverse religious standpoints: "We have a diverse spirituality in our company, and we have a very diverse spirituality in our clientele. So, it's reminding people that, oh, we can access love, we can access silence, we can access space, not everything has to be, you know."[47] This is clearly a honed vocabulary—designed to be at once mystical and shareable—one that would be immediately recognizable to most of the social business practitioners I interviewed. But in both his manner and in the content of what he was saying, Mark made it clear that being mindful was good for business. What makes you whole also makes the world whole, a little at a time.

What is bad for the world is turning your own awareness into a tool. Mark was pointedly critical of contemporary efforts to instrumentalize spirituality. At one point, I used standard language for an academic trained in structuralist analysis, asking him what function he thought spirituality played in the sector. Mark gently criticized my phrasing:

> I think one of the temptations, even in how the question is phrased, for people to think of spirituality as a tool, when it's more about how we relate to the world. It's the understanding we have of existence . . . . For myself personally and for our students and clients and for people that I know, there is of course the temptation to fall into using spiritual practices as tools. But it's really about remembering what's really important and remembering the perspective that we're approaching things . . . . It's really a sense of wholeness.[48]

Read in this way, Mark does not seek to give people mastery over their spiritual experience, but rather a humble reverence within it. He doesn't equip them to sleekly finesse their everyday professional lives through high-tech spirituality. Instead of this ethos of control and mastery, Mark leaves room for wonder, reverence, and, I think, a productive overwhelm. Like Richard, he critiques any dualism between personal wholeness and business effectiveness. Spirituality, conventionally understood, can feel like something one does on one's own time, in private, and in an inner space far removed from pedestrian concerns. But for Mark, that kind of spirituality is all too tidy and manageable, because true "spiritual practice

47. Silver, interview by author, March 29, 2019.
48. Silver, interview by author, March 29, 2019.

is everything—like, there's nothing that's not spiritual practice."[49] Being mindful of one's soul in connection to a divine source brings together everything else. It could very well be overwhelming, but the too-much-ness of it all is notably productive.

He went so far as to question the wisdom of my including a list of areas where spiritual practice might show up in a company like his. Such a list, he noted, "seems very limited." He acknowledged that my list captured common personal and organizational practices all over the place. But the problem with thinking of, say, generosity as a discrete spiritual practice, is that it makes other areas of business life seem unspiritual. What's most interesting, when looked at through a lens of spiritual capital, is that Mark allows this overwhelming sense of the divine to generate financially daring business policies. For example, he doesn't set prices for his clients, but tells them to pay what they feel they ought to.

> [P]rice setting or research and development or crafting an offer or setting policy around refunds, I mean, all of these are spiritual practices because: Are we honoring people? Are we honoring the heart? Are we honoring love? Or are we in a mind a mechanistic mindset of extraction? You see what I'm saying? Everything can remind us of the Divine.[50]

But to be reminded of God is not to be economically impractical. In fact, the overwhelming experience of God can, it seems, correct for a neglect of pragmatic concerns.

> Because a lot of our clients come to us missing really basic business skills: How do you hold a sales conversation with integrity? How do you create a marketing message that's non-manipulative but still connects with people? What's a good web strategy? What's a good business model? You know, how do you craft an offer? How do you price it? All of these basic problems that we help people solve through education.[51]

By innovating things like pricing policy, the overwhelmed awareness of the Divine that Mark seeks to inculcate unites people-care and business efficacy—a remarkably clear enactment of spiritual capital.

Tyler Etters sees his work as a vice president of the user experience and design company Highland Solutions as, in significant part, to provide an example of wellness to his colleagues. Clearly, the work of running this

49. Silver, interview by author, March 29, 2019.
50. Silver, interview by author, March 29, 2019.
51. Silver, interview by author, March 29, 2019.

small for-profit company of some 35 employees is demanding financially. And the work asks the very best efforts from Tyler as a graphic designer and creative. But, as I learned when we met for the first of several exchanges in a redwood chapel on the campus of 1440 Multiversity in Scotts Valley, California, Tyler is deeply committed to keep up an oscillatory awareness between Highland's profitability and its community's wellness. I think my dominant impression of Tyler, who might be described as an atheist with Buddhist tendencies, is that he allows his own sense of the overwhelmingness of life to propel him into people-care.

Finally, the spiritual capital of an overwhelmed awareness makes visible latent networks of care in an organization. Highland has established informal structures that make that kind of care-giving easier, something I witnessed for myself when I joined the Highland folks one day for one of their community lunches. (If I had stayed later in the afternoon, I might have caught one of their "Beer-30" afternoon gatherings as well.) But Tyler has also helped to institute formal structures to care for their employees. He and his fellow administrators did not want their employees to feel like they were being milked for all the labor they were worth, so the Highland leadership decided to allow billing for no more than 32 hours a week and to maintain communal accountability by posting the number of hours they're billing on a company dashboard. "And if you go too high over 32," Tyler added, "you're also going to hear from me, because that's not healthy. We don't want you to be working 50, 60 hours a week. If you're working 45, during a crunch time, maybe that's okay for a week or two, but you really need to be going home, spending time with your family, and disconnecting from what you do everyday."[52] Tyler is a vice president who refuses to project invulnerability.

> I talk openly about some of my anxiety concerns. I talked with a team member the other day about them. I was suffering a panic attack a week or two ago, and that's not something that leaders talk about. Leaders shouldn't have panic attacks. What are you, weak? But I could tell in her eyes that she felt comforted and validated that I shared that with her, because that gives her then permission to share with other people.[53]

For Tyler, this habit of bringing his whole self to work is a way to propagate a non-toxic work culture. Although he is clearly a highly productive graphic designer and an all-in administrator in his company, he frequently cites the mantra "people first" as a guiding value for the Highland folks.

52. Etters, interview by author, April 11, 2019.
53. Etters, interview by author, April 11, 2019.

He adds on his company blog, "In my seat as Vice President, I have the pleasure of creating digital products and experiences for the Highland team itself. And gosh, we are demanding bunch." But he takes great pleasure in the challenge: "Finding the right mix of people to work on every Highland project feels a lot like getting Tetrominoes to align — sometimes it's tough to pull off, but it's immensely satisfying when it all comes together."[54]

In the summer of 2020, I circled back to see what some of my research subjects were doing in the midst of all the breakdown and saw evidence that Tyler's company was succeeding at translating organizational wellness into organizational effectiveness. Tyler's colleague Jon Berbaum at Highland Solutions had posted a series of LinkedIn videos for helping professionals to deal with anxiety, not least through the practice of generosity. Sure enough, the Highland team had made their research data available for free via a freshly created platform called Highland Academy. The program enjoyed an impressive influx of enrollees, far more than they had hoped, and pulled in new clients for the company as well.

Jon noted to me, in a follow-up interview, that when their work slowed down to a frightening degree in the summer months, they did not fire anyone. Jon said that as a former pastor, he had been inclined to offer therapeutic support to his employees but found instead that what his team needed from him most was meaningful work. They need the wherewithal to keep moving through the world and to rejoice in the work of their hands. The Highland team allowed potentially cataclysmic conditions—global pandemic, national recession, Highland's own loss of a million dollars in contracts—to generate creative, meaningful, satisfying work to do. This work helped provide encouragement to the employees of Highland and to provide other companies with resources they could use. Productive over-whelm, indeed.[55]

The question that this form of spiritual capital leaves us with, though, is how the leader might pass it on to others. Should they, like Lady Wisdom in Proverbs, stand in the busiest hallways of the office or the most chaotic parts of the parking lot and call to all who will listen? Actually, most of the organizational leaders I spoke with tried a more dialogic approach. This next chapter examines how one-on-one conversation functions as a strategy for circulating awareness.

54. Etters, "How We Assign Members."
55. Mattson, "Household Economics at Highland Solutions—Jon Berbaum."

3

Moving from Dialogue to Multilogue

For the moment, we face each other across this page as a You and an I, each agreeing to the ancient contract of reader and writer. I take it as a good omen that you're still here, although I suspect it would be less work and more fun for both of us simply to sit down and have a conversation. You are no doubt well-practiced in conversation, especially if, like so many of the leaders I've interviewed for this project, you often find yourself investing in dialogue with coworkers. Do you have team members distracted from what the organization's all about? Are some employees too focused on their own tasks so that they've lost the big picture? Is the pursuit of organizational mission burning out some of your folks? Faced with the sometimes-tensioned goals of effectiveness and wellness, in other words, the instrument that leaders reach for is dialogue.

I found this emphasis on the vitality of conversation again and again in my research. Frequent, honest, searching conversations in a workplace community can correct for the worst blind spots of managerialism, reduce the possibility of passive spectatorship among employees, and generate creative problem-solving. Let me cite a few examples. Amor Montes de Oca describes her work at the incubator 2112 in terms of close, patient, knowing conversations. "We have an understanding of where each of our entrepreneurs are, and we have a two-way channel where they can come to us and say, 'I am overwhelmed' or 'I'm lost.' And we will find a mentor or a way for the entrepreneur to be able to unclog that bottleneck so that they can continue."[1] Sarah Woolsey of the Impact Guild likes to use dialogic imagery in her description of her work, where she believes "it very naturally opens up the conversations to people's motivations and why they're driven to find meaning and purpose." Her experience suggests to her "that there *is* something uniquely spiritual and uniquely, I would say, tied to the thing that God has put in our hearts, even if a lot of people aren't naming it as such."[2] For Sarah as for many people, interpersonal dialogue gives access within a working community to people's inner lives. Laura Zumdahl talks about regular dialogues called "Pizza and God," which her company hosts. She describes them as "a totally optional time" for people to "bring any questions they have about faith" and discuss them with a spiritual director.[3] I have written at length elsewhere about the use of dialogic interaction for consultancy, especially at companies like Lime Red Studio, where instead of presenting clients with extensive quantitative evidence right up front, Emily Lonigro and Demetrio Maguigad move first into an hours-long dialogue, exploring issues that the company might not have realized even about its own mission.[4]

Those are just four examples. But I hardly need cite more: the indispensable social and spiritual value of workplace conversation constitutes taken-for-granted wisdom in organizational management today. "In certain quarters dialogue has attained something of a holy status," communication scholar John Durham Peters observes. "It is held up as the summit of human encounter, the essence of liberal education and the medium of participatory democracy."[5] In many organizational communities, "having a conversation" enacts a much-admired vision for personal formation and social practice, addressing desires both for individual growth and communal equity.

Still, optimistic assumptions about the possibilities of heart-to-heart connection warrants more careful examination than we usually give it, as I will suggest in the case study to follow.[6] Ultimately, the goal for this chapter

1. Montes de Oca, interview by author, April 5, 2019.
2. Woolsey, interview by author, March 27, 2019.
3. Zumdahl, interview by author, January 25, 2019.
4. Mattson, *Rethinking Communication*, 95–98.
5. Peters, *Speaking into the Air*, 33.
6. For thoughtful discussion in a vein akin to this chapter, see theorists like Taylor and Deetz, who have cast egalitarian workplace conversations as essential to contemporary business life. See Taylor, "Dialogue as the Search," 125–60. Well-conducted dialogue "clearly continues as a social hope as we confront the problems of a new era," write Deetz and Simpson in "Critical Organizational Dialogue," 141. Deetz and Simpson, although they recommend dialogue in organizational life, are alert to the naïve assumptions about "spiritual connection" via disclosive conversation that I am critiquing in this chapter.

is to make visible yet another form of spiritual capital, which I will call *mutual circulation*. True mutuality and genuine circulation are indispensable goods in the life of an organization, but they can be hard to spot and hard to activate.[7] Some of their hiddenness is due to the picture in our heads for what Having a Conversation means. The pace and profusion of contemporary messaging make us wish for a "spiritual" connection between one inner self and another, when we should be hoping instead for the practical business that J. L. Austin's famous book title summed as "how to do things with words."[8] After discussing conversational breakdown and organizational breakout in the enterprise Matryoshka Haus, I turn to the book of Job, a wisdom story that clarifies, by its simplicity, its eloquence, and its distance from our own confusing time, what we should hope for as we try with others to do things with words.

CASE STUDY: WHEN CONVERSATION'S NOT ENOUGH

People called Shannon Hopkins a missionary long after the term no longer described her. They should have called her a social entrepreneur, a better description of the work she'd left the United States to do in London. On the 200th anniversary of the passage of the anti-slavery law by William Wilberforce, she and a small team launched an awareness-raising campaign called The Truth Isn't Sexy (TTIS), eventually recruiting a coalition of six-thousand religiously disenfranchised young people. Shannon and her team spread out across the United Kingdom, tossing provocative beer mats on pub counters: the coasters featured erotic imagery on one side and on the other, brutal facts about sex trafficking. The campaign garnered research data, won impressive awards, and directed the national conversation away from "rescuing" women and towards the male consumers actually driving the trade.[9] But when Shannon reported this good news to her churchly donors back in the States, she lost fifty percent of her support. Despite all the clear impact, despite the engagement with otherwise religiously disaffected

---

7. My own reflection on mutuality is shaped by three sources. Webb, *The Gifting God*: Webb helped me to see that *some* kind of exchange is not inimical to generosity in community. Mark Sampson, "The Promise of Social Enterprise": Not only was Mark one of my research subjects, but he was also, through his dissertation, a teacher to me. His reading of John Barclay in particular helped me to make sense of the mutuality of community without reducing it to tight reciprocity. Barclay, *Paul & the Gift*, 363–65: Barclay helped me understand the history of the concept of grace and what it has to do with the circulation of cultural capital in communities.

8. Austin, *How To Do Things*.

9. "The Truth isn't Sexy," Matryoshka Haus.

youth, Shannon's work didn't fit into the available categories for missional work. Where were the converts, the baptisms? Also, the campaign's erotic messaging didn't fit the aesthetic of a church bulletin.

Shannon decided to switch from the mass communications of awareness-raising to the interpersonal communication of entrepreneurial incubation, founding the accelerator Matryoshka Haus in 2009. The social innovators Shannon recruited resulted in instruments for measurable social impact—well before impact assessment had entered common parlance.[10] These creatives quickly showed themselves skilled at playful, generative dialogue. Matryoshka was eventually managing six distinct business models with clients on two continents.

But by the time I interviewed Shannon in 2019 for this book, Matryoshka had started to bleed. Shannon was understandably guarded about airing her organizational crises in our first conversation—and, I think, she felt rather bewildered by the organization's predicament, which was partly interpersonal and partly infrastructural. "We were working harder and harder and harder," she explained to me in a later conversation, "and it wasn't feeling any better than when we were bootstrapping in the beginning. And so, it was like, something's not really working."[11] Shannon's colleagues outside the organization were starting to put a blunt forefinger on Matryoshka's organizational conversations. Their creative dialogues couldn't compensate for the essential work of organizational infrastructure. "You guys are always going to do new things, and it comes out of your vocation," their friends told them. "But if you're really going to have a healthy org, you really need someone to help you, the way you guys help others." The Matryoshka team had a hard time denying the truth in this. Having grown explosively, the organization was spiritually overleveraged.

Shannon knew her colleagues to be "some very bright people," highly skilled at problem-solving conversation. "We could have just made something happen." But she wasn't convinced they *should* talk their way through and out of this crisis. Instead, the Matryoshka team chose, as Shannon later put it, to "reclaim our spiritual capital."[12] The process didn't feel very

10. Their Transformation Index (TI) is still in use, although the rest of the conversation on social impact assessment continues nascent. The TI gamifies the process with 56 descriptors on playing cards, which teams sort through, gradually eliminating those indicators that do not fit their company mission and selecting five apt descriptors for themselves. Regarding the immaturity of the impact assessment conversation more generally, Cole, et. al offers this encouraging, but perspective-setting word, that "the financial accounting standards, upon which investors rely, took decades to develop." Cole, et al., "Background Note."

11. Mattson, "Good Grief and Organizational Change—Shannon Hopkins."

12. Mattson, "Good Grief and Organizational Change—Shannon Hopkins."

spiritual: they hired a managing partner and conducted a stringent self-review, ultimately deciding to break up their organization into smaller entities. Shannon felt the pain acutely. "2019 is not a year I'd want to redo," she told me in a voice heavy with tears. "There was a lot of pain and suffering and, 'Are we going to get through it and are we going to get through it and love one another still? Be happy? Be content? Have a hope for what comes next?'"[13]

I share this case study, because it highlights, among other things, the limits of interpersonal conversation as a guiding approach to organizational work. Incubators like Matryoshka, of course, rely heavily on face-to-face dialoguing among team members, with clients, and with community members. Having interviewed Shannon's close colleagues, Cathers Pearson and Mark Sampson, I can attest that the one-on-one model of organizational communication has conspicuous virtues. What they had to say about their work, assumes an organizational ethos of egalitarianism, shared responsibility, an approach to workplace life that is open to fresh ideas and challenging questions. One of Shannon's great fears when Matryoshka subdivided was they might not "get through it and love one another still"—which suggests a fear of losing the warmhearted interactions of the company.[14] As her own story suggests, however, workplaces require more than impassioned, ideational dialogue. Such conversations are essential to some parts of organizational life, but not sufficient for sustainable organizational futures.

There are good, historical reasons for this privileging of interpersonal conversation as a way to negotiate professional organizations. Think of the long and storied liberal arts tradition, and you probably call books to mind. But bookish communication has made up only the left channel, so to speak, in the cabling of Western thought. The right channel has, as far back as Plato, been the practice of dialogue. In his dialogue *Phaedrus*, for example, Plato dramatizes two conversationalists, Socrates and Phaedrus, thinking about what makes for good and wise relationships. In a bid to draw Phaedrus into a richly awakened way of life, Socrates disabuses the young man of impersonal relationships and draws him instead to enter into thoughtful and impassioned dialogue. Plato would be skeptical that the book you are holding right now enables wisdom. Why? Because words on a page "are as incapable of speaking in their own defense as they are of teaching the truth adequately."[15] That very conviction that the best things come from back-and-forth-ness in intimate conversation entailed that my interview subjects,

13. Mattson, "Good Grief and Organizational Change—Shannon Hopkins."
14. Mattson, "Good Grief and Organizational Change—Shannon Hopkins."
15. Plato, *Phaedrus*, 276c.

without ever citing a Platonic dialogue, nonetheless embrace his counsels for impassioned, insightful conversation.

A great part of why we value face-to-face dialogue so much is the widely held conviction that our technologized society has disabled authentic interaction. We feel ourselves to be, as Kenneth Burke put it, "separated from [our] natural condition by instruments of [our] own making."[16] But as Peters's "history of the idea of communication" has shown, moderns learned to long for authentic, face-to-face communication precisely as a result of witnessing the seemingly magical conducting of electronic interchange. When the telegraph first showed up, people witnessed a mode of transmission that seemed well-nigh spiritual in its effortlessness. "Interpersonal relations gradually became redescribed in the technical terms of transmission at a distance—making contact, tuning in or out, being on the same wavelength, getting good or bad vibes, or 'Earth to Herbert, come in please!'"[17] Of course, the potential for what we wryly call technical difficulties—emails getting sent to spam, microphones not plugged in, Wi-Fi disconnects—have also prompted us to think that interpersonal communication really ought to be free of such disruptions. Peters sums up his argument by saying, "Communication as a person-to-person activity became thinkable only in the shadow of mediated communication . . . Miscommunication is the scandal that motivates the very concept of communication in the first place."[18] When we find ourselves baffled by an email that did not go through or a notification that mysteriously fails to notify, we can hardly help longing for a good, old-fashioned heart-to-heart chat. But what if Peters is right to say that our "notion of communication deserves to be liberated from its earnestness and spiritualism, its demand for precision and agreement"?[19] What we will need instead is a spiritual capital that enables genuine mutuality and practical circulation—without insisting on a linkage of soul to soul.

I think we can find advice for finding such capital in a dialogue older than Plato's, the book of Job, whose dialogue enacts a breakdown in interpersonal conversation. This failure of dialogue as a social tool reveals the shortcomings of another piece of moral technology—quid pro quo retributionism. Theologians call this the retributionist policy, in which everyone is always rewarded for good actions and punished for bad. Using this moral technology has come to shape what they expect in their interactions with each other and with God. When both this moral principle and its attendant

16. Burke, "Definition of Man," 16.

17. Peters, *Speaking into the Air*, 5.

18. Peters, *Speaking into the Air*, 6.

19. Peters, *Speaking into the Air*, 31.

mode of dialogue breaks down, the story pulls Job out of the tight reciprocity of interpersonal dialogue and into the mutuality of a community's multilogue.

DIALOGUE & REWARD

This is a poem, as all the world knows, about a good man in hard pain. Job's wealth has been destroyed, his children killed, his health decimated, and for no discernible reason. Thinking about the book of Job in connection with the interviews of this book helped me notice that a lot of my research subjects spoke from histories of deep pain. They described days of trauma when their hair fell out, when panic attacks set in, when identities fissured and even fractured. They spoke of years they'd never want to live again, of having to shut down enterprises, of needing to fire someone, of having to euthanize their own organizational model. They talked of whole communities shaped by systemic inequity and oppression. Job's experience of undeserved trauma helps bring to attention the woundedness that so often shapes organizational life.

"Have you noticed my friend Job?" asks God to the satan figure who appears before a poetically imagined divine court room near the beginning of the book. "There's no one quite like him—honest and true to his word, totally devoted to God and hating evil."[20] The satan is the wittiest and most sharply spoken character in the first chapters of the Job poem; he may also be the most distracted. When asked where he's been, the satan answers blandly, "From going to and fro on the earth, and from walking up and down on it."[21] When asks if he's thought much about Job, the satan does not answer directly, perhaps because he has been too distracted in his wanderings to notice. Instead, he asks a counter question: "Does Job fear God for nothing?"[22]

The satan's question is uncomfortable, but it compels renewed attention to how Job is described in the first lines of the book:

> There was once a man in the land of Uz whose name was Job. That man was blameless and upright, one who feared God and turned away from evil. There were born to him seven sons and three daughters. He had seven thousand sheep, three thousand camels, five hundred yoke of oxen, five hundred

---

20. Job 1:8 MSG.
21. Job 1:7 NRSV.
22. Job 1:9 NRSV.

donkeys, and very many servants; so that this man was the greatest of all the people of the east.[23]

The implicit linkage of his god-fearing ways and his great wealth appears to underwrite his social capital as well. We learn later, from Job's own mournful testimony, that, before all the misfortune, the most veteran of citizens would defer to him; the youngest would keep silence whenever he spoke. This respect was well-deserved. We learn, both from what his friends say and what he himself notes, that he has been a philanthropist, unfailingly generous to those who have suffered loss. He is also a law-and-order man, not the sort that perpetrators wished to cross in court.

The writer of the book makes sure in the framing narrative at the start of the book to note that Job is a person of rigorous spiritual practice. Besides managing all his economic capital, Job also keeps close moral accounts, praying copiously for his children's wellbeing. They held banquets in each other's homes for days on end, at the end of which Job made a practice of balancing out their moral bookkeeping:

> And when the feast days had run their course, Job would send and sanctify them, and he would rise early in the morning and offer burnt offerings according to the number of them all; for Job said, "It may be that my children have sinned, and cursed God in their hearts." This is what Job always did.[24]

The man seems to recognize that with his great wealth comes vulnerability and accountability. Accordingly, he maintains a scrupulosity not only about his own behavior but about others', as well. For much of his life, little has happened to question his sense that the moral universe has responded commensurately to his upright way of life.

But the satan's query expresses an unlooked-for fissure in the mainstream wisdom traditions upon which Job was relying. These teachings sometimes insisted on the so-called retribution principle, that those who do what is right will be rewarded and those who do what is wrong will be punished. As Lindsay Wilson sums it, "According to this theory, punishment should be administered *only* when it is deserved, and then only to the extent that it is deserved . . . The basic principle is: Whatever a person deserves, that should be their punishment, no more or no less."[25]

When the satan challenges the integrity of Job, the Almighty accepts the challenge and gives permission to divest Job of all his property and even

---

23. Job 1:1–3 NRSV.
24. Job 1:5 NRSV.
25. Wilson, *Job*, 219–20.

to kill his children. Job's response to this economic and personal calamity is to pay out still more spiritual attentiveness: he responds to his trouble by worshipping God.

> Then Job arose, tore his robe, shaved his head, and fell on the ground and worshiped. He said, "Naked I came from my mother's womb, and naked shall I return there; the Lord gave, and the Lord has taken away; blessed be the name of the Lord."[26]

Most readers have seen in these words an enormous resilience and greatness in Job's soul, but there may also be something a little conventional about this maxim, a certain patness in his phrasing, a stubborn confidence that the economic arrangements of the moral universe might yet be put right. Perhaps, we can imagine Job saying, *This is a test, and soon all will be put right, if only I can maintain integrity.* In any case, the satan continues to be skeptical and presses God to let him strike Job again, this time with a terrible skin disease. Job responds with yet more attentiveness: he sets aside all maxims and practices silence for seven days. So far, Job has acted with the sort of greatness of soul that his three visiting friends, Eliphaz, Bildad, and Zophar, would have expected of him.

What comes next, though, in Job's first speech is an agonized cry as deep and as pained as any in any wisdom literature. He howls his wish to be unmade, to never have been created. Accusing God of distending the retribution principle, Job theorizes that perhaps God is punishing him overzealously. He asks for reprieve from oppressive surveillance:

> What are human beings, that you make so much of them,
> that you sent your mind on them,
> visit them every morning,
> test them every moment.
> Will you not look away from me for a while,
> let me alone until I swallow my spittle?
> If I sin, what do I do to you, you watcher of humanity?
> Why have you made me your target?[27]

Most of the time, though, Job asks not for a lessening, but for a tightening of divine attentiveness. His most common request is for a face-to-face argument with God so that they can argue out what has happened to Job point by point. The retributionist principle he had wielded all his life has broken down; he hopes to restore it through the give and take of forensic

26. Job 1:20–21 NRSV.
27. Job 7:17–20 NRSV.

debate. He does not yet see that the breakdown of the retributionist equipment points to the inadequacy of a face-to-face forensic dialogue as well.

Nor do his friends see things any more clearly. They hammer him with their favorite theory of justice. Eliphaz begins gently enough, almost hesitant to speak. But even he cuts to the point, that the sufferer must have committed some wrongdoing, that the sufferer must somehow deserve this catastrophe. As Eliphaz asks in his first speech,

> Think now, who that was innocent ever perished?
> Or where were the upright cut off?[28]

As if Job through a massive obliviousness must have forgotten his own wrongdoing, Zophar urges,

> If iniquity is in your hand, put it far away,
> and do not let wickedness reside in your tents.
> Surely then you will lift up your face without blemish;
> you will be secure and will not fear.
> You will forget your misery;
> you will remember it as waters that have passed away.[29]

But the moral technology of the retribution principle, although it is landing blows on Job, fails to change his mind. He agrees, after all, with his friends on how the universe is supposed to work; he differs only on whether it *is* working that way. They all see life as an exchange with the universe, in which pious attention to God's commandments pays prosperity in full. Able to check the ledgers of a lifetime of careful moral accountability, Job knows that something is not right. In one of the most heartbreaking lines of the book, Job asks them, "But now, be pleased to look at me"[30] —as if to say, "You know me, you know my life, and you should know I don't deserve this!" But they prove incapable of even this most elemental expectation of ethical conversation, to see the other as she or he actually is.

In most of his speeches, Job begins by refuting his friends and then directing his complaint to the Almighty. Although he grows steadily angrier with his friends, he keeps hoping for a better exchange with God.

> Look, my eye has seen all this,
> my ear has heard and understood it.
> What you know, I also know;
> I am not inferior to you.

---

28. Job 4:7 NRSV.

29. Job 11:14–16 NRSV.

30. Job 6:28 NRSV.

> But I would speak to the Almighty,
>   and I desire to argue my case with God.
> As for you, you whitewash with lies;
>   all of you are worthless physicians.
> If you would only keep silent,
>   that would be your wisdom![31]

The dialogue grows tedious, as the speeches lengthen and repeat themselves. And that tediousness itself is telling. Something about the moral technology being used over and over again is faulty, although neither Job, his friends, nor we (at least within the world of the story) can quite make out what's not working.

DIALOGUE WITH THE UNIVERSE

In my conversations with organizational leaders, I often found a similar linkage between people's conversational expectations of the moral universe. For many organizational consultants, it wasn't just the case that dialogue was essential to good workplace effectiveness and wellbeing, but also that it was somehow essential to deep structures in the universe. The world is fundamentally dialogic.

When Bryan Ungard and I spoke, he was fingering a pair of tiger-eye bracelets, and, when I asked him about them, told me a story about the DMV. He had been late for an appointment and had expected the worst. But there had been no line, and the young man behind the counter actually apologized for taking a bare minute to process his form. Bryan complimented his tiger-eye bracelet, and without a moment's hesitation, the DMV attendant slipped it off his wrist and handed it to Bryan. Although people usually wear tiger-eye stones to stave off anxiety, Bryan wears it to remind himself not to be too deferential to his own fears. "And maybe," he added, "I should be open to the world unfolding in ways I don't expect it to."[32] Bryan's story seemed like a tossed-off anecdote at first. But after the third time re-listening to his interview, I began to think that his openness to surprising interactions with the world was emblematic of the way he asks questions of his life.

Perhaps the most striking question that Bryan asked pertained not to himself or to the selves of his stakeholders, but to the "self" of his company. Organizations, like people, have what he called an "essence" and not just a brand expression. This essence is shaped by the company's ecology, where it finds itself. Organizational essence is also shaped by what the company

31. Job 13:1–5 NRSV.

32. Ungard, interview by author, April 12, 2019.

has had to do in order to persist and flourish. People within the company can discern their organizational soul by asking thoughtful conversational questions very like the ones Bryan asked of himself and his employees. The world and the self and the other all welcome and respond to our conversational inquiry.

Other people I spoke with took a similarly dialogic stance. Jon Cordas began our conversation about his work as a life and work consultant by talking about a TED Talk that thousands of people have celebrated: Simon Sinek's account of the Golden Circle. Sinek's plan for discernment, Jon explained, is highly popular and generally effective at least on an individual level. The method helps you discern what animates a person, what motivates, what calls. But when it comes to helping a *company* to discern a shared calling, the Golden Circle is something less than golden. "It is not sufficient, people discover, for highly collaborative alternative operating systems or governance systems."[33] For that, Cordas recommends what he calls a Direct Access Method, which essentially involves having a conversation with Whatever's Out There.

Jon is the first to acknowledge that his approach to organizational discernment strikes some people as more than a little uncanny. Although the facilitators of this method *can* use non-spiritual terminology, the method relies upon an understanding of humans as essentially spiritual beings in a tightly interactive relationship with the world. The procedure works like this. People gather for a large-scale meeting. They individually determine what their reliable source of wisdom will be. They are collectively given a discernment question, sometimes a fiercely contested question, one that admits of no easy answers. (Jon goes so far as to say that Direct Access Methods are for impossible questions, questions made impossible by a fractious team or by a seemingly insurmountable task.) Each member in the group—and sometimes the groups gathered may number in the many hundreds—then puts the question to their source. Then they take careful notes on what they hear.

Jon's conviction that our moral inquiry will be rewarded with the wisdom we seek from the universe we live in made me uncomfortable. My own background in teaching rhetoric made me worry that such methods of collective discernment devalue what seem to me indispensable roles for citizenly argument, deliberation, and debate. But Jon, noting that the boardrooms of the world are often choked by such arguments, recommends sticking with a conversation with the universe.[34]

33. Cordas, interview by author, April 22, 2019.
34. Cordas, interview by author, April 22, 2019.

Like Jon, Andy Swindler uses a program (developed by Tim Kelley) he calls True Purpose, to help organizational leaders to cultivate partnership between their egos and some sort of higher consciousness. Andy does not critique the ego, telling people to stop being selfish. This, he suggests, can result in "a game of whack a mole" in which "we're shoving it further down in the subconscious . . . and it's going to show up somewhere else."[35] True personal liberation comes, he believes, when we speak to ourselves honestly and attentively. "I'll coach people to literally have a dialogue with their inner critic."[36] The ego, after all, is alert to the basic needs of human life, sometimes in a way that higher consciousness can be rather cavalier about. But ultimately, Andy wants to help facilitate dialogue between his clients and whatever they hold to be a "trusted source," which does not entail ignoring the ego but rather cultivating a working relationship with it. Andy is really into dialogic accounts of reality. For him, our trusted source might be anything from a divine being to a numerical figure to a piece of desk equipment. "If that stapler knows your purpose, then you're going to be talking to that stapler. It's an energy field. So basically, interview it."[37] Andy's humor here is representative of a larger commitment in his work with True Purpose to the vitality of play in well-lived human life. But it also speaks to his sense that we do not control reality but attend to it and converse with it.

As with Jon's collective practices of spiritual discernment, Andy explains that a great benefit of the True Purpose model is that it enables corporate decision-making. He describes working with seven different leaders at a manufacturing company through a discernment process: "They all have different trusted sources, and they're all to be accessing those trusted sources in the room together in a workshop in April to gather information about the company's purpose."[38] At times, they sound like qualitative researchers coding the data they receive from the spirit world. When I ask him what happens when some of those manufacturers believe their trusted source is God, while others believe (as Andy himself seems to) that it is simply intuition, he shrugs and smiles.

> Because even when they're all together, they're still accessing their different trusted source. It might even be a different trusted source. Maybe God is able to tell them their personal purpose. But actually, their dead Aunt Martha is the one who, for whatever reason, coming up over the spirit world, understands the

35. Swindler, interview by author, February 15, 2019.
36. Swindler, interview by author, February 15, 2019.
37. Swindler, interview by author, February 15, 2019.
38. Swindler, interview by author, February 15, 2019.

purpose of the business. So that's part of the process is, actually, make sure they've all—they're all talking to a trusted source that understands the business purpose.[39]

I have found in these interviews about organizational spirituality that, when talking about spirituality, there frequently is a moment where people have to concede that the thing they are describing sounds fringy. Jon acknowledges that what these teams and organizations hear individually and then report collectively can be quite eerie. "And what you find in the boardroom when you use a direct access method is people will receive very similar answers. And the word that comes up most often in the use of it is spooky. Because they're all getting the same stuff."[40] His words about spookiness reminded me of Eliphaz's claim to have received the wisdom he is giving to Job from an uncanny source:

> Now a word came stealing to me,
>   my ear received the whisper of it.
> Amid thoughts from visions of the night,
>   when deep sleep falls on mortals,
>   dread came upon me, and trembling,
>   which made all my bones shake.[41]

Andy's rhetorical strategy for dealing with the discomfort of this uncanniness is, unlike Eliphaz, to resort to playful metaphor: he makes it sound as if the trusted source that is Aunt Martha is getting picked up through an unencrypted Wi-Fi network. Tyler Etters agreed that people often reach a point in describing how they see the world where they are forced to concede that they might sound a little wacky. "I think that that clause 'I know this sounds crazy' is kind of like a code for 'Just reminding you we're humans and we don't know everything,' or reminding you to check your paradigms, check what you think you know as the absolute truth, and acknowledge that your perceptions are different than my perceptions."[42] But for most people, I think, the admission of fringiness is a nod to the uncanny responsiveness of Being.

What Jon and Andy and others of my research subjects expressed amounted to what David Whyte has called a "conversational view of reality."[43] Unlike the sometimes grim worldview of Job and his friends, this

---

39. Swindler, interview by author, February 15, 2019.
40. Cordas, interview by author, April 22, 2019.
41. Job 4:12–14 NRSV.
42. Etters, interview by author, April 11, 2019.
43. I encountered this phrase in Tippett, "The Conversational Nature of Reality."

take on ultimate things can be quite humorous and humble and practical. Reality cannot be engineered to suit us. In fact, in Whyte's understanding, this worldview entails constant transformation of the person dialoguing with Being. Talk with the universe, and you will be changed—and so will the universe, at least a little. Whyte seems relatively uninterested in the retributionist principle that so preoccupies Job. At the same time, Whyte's worldview appears to embrace what might be called an attributionist principle. Instead of emphasizing that people are punished according to their deserts, he affirms that if we converse with the world, we will ultimately be rewarded in some way or another. The conversation may be uncomfortable and will likely put us off balance, but eventually we will be rewarded with a kind of wisdom and acceptance and joy.

For Whyte, the rewards of dialogue with the universe is usually insight. For the people I interviewed, the rewards might be insight—or business success. Andy's confidence, for example, that the universe rewards people who engage reality fearlessly is grounded in his own experience of seeing people "land on their truth" and prosper in their business.[44] "The world responds—economically," he insists.[45]

> The times when I convinced myself, that's not something somebody wants to hear is when I'm letting my own shadow hold me back. So part of it is just the generic, we need capital, and part of it is that I would ask every single one of those people, Are you living your truth? Are you embodied in your truth and your purpose from a place of love. That I think is what's actually going to lead us to this next innovation.[46]

Approaching the world conversationally and experimentally, much in the way one would approach coworkers for an important exchange, is for many organizational leaders a way to enact mindfulness, a way to unite business strategy and community care.

Testimonials to the beneficial results of such interactions filled my notebooks. Bryan insists that committing to "something that's bigger than the group, that's bigger than them" means that "different results happen. You don't have to work on the results. They just happen. In this case, different business results happen."[47] Maiken Piil talks about using her own life as a

---

Whyte works out the implications of this view of reality in a series of meditations in *Consolations.*

44. Swindler, interview by author, February 15, 2019.
45. Swindler, interview by author, February 15, 2019.
46. Swindler, interview by author, February 15, 2019.
47. Ungard, interview by author, April 12, 2019.

kind of laboratory where she tries out experiments for how to avoid burnout and how to make more money with less effort.

> And I feel it's like a constant flow for learning and for align-ing myself with the day and for manifesting results, business, and keeping myself in alignment, so that business opportunities come in. And I'm experiencing, in my own journey, I have to do less and less. It's like this weird thing: the less I do, the more opportunities just pop into my inbox.[48]

These organizational leaders bear witness to a kind of moral structure to the universe: if you approach the world as a conversation partner, surprising results will happen. Some, like Maiken see this relationship as a fairly tight quid pro quo relation.

Others seem to see the karmic principle as being a looser generality. For Corey Kohn, for instance, the world's responsiveness wasn't something that surfaced often in our conversations. She describes herself somewhat cheerfully as a "Jew-Bu"—Jewish and Buddhist.[49] She described a charac-teristically post-secular journey in social entrepreneurship as an alternative expression of religious vocation. It was illuminating to figure out that "the world can be healed" not only by extraordinary heroism, but by ordinary work in an ordinary company.[50] "I can use this thing—which is business and commerce—and actually use that, instead of just rejecting it out of hand, and joining the convent or going into retreat or whatever it is."[51] Corey, in turn, benefits, as her company enacts value that, in her words "feeds me on a spiritual level."[52] But Corey's wisdom-seeking entailed a view of the world that resisted the logic of the market, the reduction of every value and every relation to a commodity. Although she was convinced that sometimes taking a risk in this world brings good energy, she worried about a secular prosperity gospel that "feeds people this sense of, oh, if I just do those things, if I just follow my breath and I just eat vegetarian and I just blah blah blah, then I will be a happy person. And the answer to that is absolutely not."[53] But still, she does seem to see some sort of conversational relationship with reality: she tells the story, for example, of how, when her company DOJO4,

---

48. Piil, interview by author, April 3, 2019.
49. Kohn, interview by author, May 10, 2019.
50. Kohn, interview by author, May 10, 2019.
51. Kohn, interview by author, May 10, 2019.
52. Kohn, interview by author, May 10, 2019.
53. Kohn, interview by author, May 10, 2019.

switched to a social enterprise model, "right away, there was this influx of energy, good feelings. We got way more interesting clients."[54]

Emily Lonigro gives perhaps the most vivid expression I've encountered of this hopefulness regarding the universe's moral arc:

> And then you just do it and you're like, something will happen. We don't know what it is, but we know at least we did the right thing and that's sometimes—when we had a dark year like last year, I was, like, we're just going to keep going, because statistically this will work out and also it never hasn't worked out. And in fifteen years, it's never not worked out. So, we're going to do it and it's going to be fine and just—And one day I, you know, I just said it out loud, and then we, like, closed two jobs that day . . . [W]hen you really concentrate and really manifest it, when you do it, it works. It works all the time.[55]

CONVERSATION IS NOT ENOUGH

Three quarters of the way through the book of Job, the dialogue has reached its end. The friends have come to the end of their attempt to confirm their karmic-conversational view of reality. No more maxims or cries remain. They have also come to the end of their attentiveness for each other. I imagine them sitting on the ground before a burned-out shell of the house. There are broken tree branches everywhere. They all have bits of ash on their hands, their shoulders, their bald heads. Job is covered in lesions that he scratches now and again with a shard of clay. Three of the men are wearing black; Job wears little except a blanket someone has thrown over him. He sits mute, as do the others, dull-eyed with the heavy sense that speech and attention can do nothing more. Their silence now is broken only by the sound of stone scraping skin.

The next person to break the silence is Elihu, apparently a nearby listener to the speechmaking of Job and his friends. He's a young, impertinent speaker, but a charismatic one, someone who speaks because he is pent up with the effort of trying to be still. He compares himself to a wine bottle about to burst. Like Job, Elihu really wants Job to hear God's speaking; unlike Job, he imagines this speech coming from all directions—not just arriving in one-on-one dialogue but arriving in community and within all of creation. Elihu maintains a complex theology, a mixture of optimism about

---

54. Kohn, interview by author, May 10, 2019.

55. Lonigro, interview by author, June 20, 2017.

moral action and a profound sense of the mysteriousness of the world where we find ourselves.

Tyler was something of an Elihu, albeit a Buddhist atheistic version of that character. He was resistant to the taken-for-granted wisdom of many social entrepreneurs that the universe responds positively to positive moral action. "I emphatically, categorically, and completely reject the idea that the arc of history bends towards justice, or that there is some good, benevolent guiding force that responds generously to magnanimous projects."[56] For him, a conversation with the universe might better be understood as a conversation with oneself—we create our own meaningfulness—and with one's workplace community. After praising his company's president for taking the organization (Highland Solutions) in a missional direction, Tyler said,

> [A]ll the Highlanders are just, we're so totally excited about it. I so rarely use the word "we" because I don't like taking more than my responsibility when speaking for the company, but everyone is so stoked to be working on, like I mentioned, the Morton Arboretum or the Children's Hospital, all these things are actually making the world better. And it's like, I've freelanced for a long time, I've worked at a lot of other companies. The difference at the end of the day when you go home between working on a project, a piece of software, an integration for a company that you don't really believe in or you don't really care about, versus one that you know is going to do something and help people and maybe make them be able to leave work an hour early so they can go home and spend time with their family—it's like night and day. It's a completely different experience, and I don't even really have words for how much better you feel.[57]

Tyler holds two notions—that life is pointless and that humans can create significance—which he believes make optimism a viable stance in our cultural moment. He speaks of a "sense of mystery and wonder" as a live option, even though "a lot of people don't know that it's even there," due to the fact that "being cynical is cool now."[58] He himself embraces a kind

---

56. Etters, email message to author, September 30, 2019.

57. Etters, interview by author, April 12, 2019.

58. He says that people born in his time (the late-80s) often send each other "cynically resigned and ironically pessimistic" memes about how the destruction of the natural world and the end of democracy. "They're frickin hysterical; they're really funny, but it's just like the default posture is this resignation that nothing is gonna change, nothing is gonna get better." Etters, interview by author, April 12, 2019.

of attitude towards the universe that might best be described as nihilistic optimism.[59]

Another Elihu I encountered along the way, someone voicing uneasiness with the notion that history can be repaired by a simple conversation with the universe, was Rosa Lee Harden, a long-time leader in the social impact investment space and the co-founder of SOCAP. One thing I learned from her was that what looks like a successful conversation *with* the world just might not be good *for* the world. She noted about social impact investment, "People did it for great reasons, but some people got really rich on it. So then, what do you do with that?"[60] Now that big venture capital funds are entering the social impact realm, Rosa Lee asks if social entrepreneurs might be "just making more money for rich people to have more money."[61] A second and related pitfall is to believe that there is a kind of divinely appointed inevitability to personal and historical progress. Rosa Lee critiques this attitude towards history under the aegis of the Prosperity Gospel, the notion that if we live good and godly lives, we will be providentially blessed. She insists that "the Prosperity Gospel's a bitch, and she's gonna get us. She is coming at us. The prosperity gospel is killing this country. The people think that the more you have the more you're blessed."[62]

But although Elihu gets the wisdom of the dialogue part way home, he is not quite able to consummate the insight the book has yet to give. Elihu is giving a bit of breathing room between the claustrophobic quarters of Job's dialogue with his friends and the whirlwind that is about to come.[63]

FROM DIALOGUE TO MULTILOGUE

The final poetry from the whirlwind in the Book of Job sounds at first like it will be a conversation, as the Almighty invites response from Job:

> Gird up your loins like a man,
> I will question you, and you shall declare to me.[64]

---

59. I'm grateful to Ben Hoekstra for suggesting this phrase to me.

60. Harden, interview by author, May 30, 2019.

61. Harden, interview by author, May 30, 2019.

62. Harden, interview by author, May 30, 2019.

63. Wilson says that the speeches "of Elihu set the reader free from observing the dilemma solely through Job's eyes." Elihu's word "provides space between Job's summons and God's appearance, so that God is not seen as at Job's beck and call." Wilson, *Job*, 157.

64. Job 38:3 NRSV.

But this encounter with God startles Job into an awed silence. All the way through the book, Job has been demanding God's attention, has wanted to enter into an exchange in which so and so much human attention would be rewarded by so and so much divine reciprocity. Job has hoped that he could find rectification for all his pain and loss by an attentive reassessment from God as judge. But Job doesn't find the courtroom; instead the courtroom, in the form of a massive storm, finds him. And from the midst of that storm, God speaks, not in the sort of tidily two-way mode Job's retributionism had led him to imagine, but overwhelmingly and from every direction. "I will question you, and you shall declare to me," says God, adding later, "Anyone who argues with God must respond." But Job's longing for tightly reciprocal conversation—in which each person takes their turn to make their case—looks wholly inadequate in the midst of a whirlwind of questions:

Who is this that darkens counsel by words without knowledge? . . .

Can you bind the chains of the Pleiades,
    or loose the cords of Orion? . . .

Can you hunt the prey for the lion,
    or satisfy the appetite of the young lions,
when they crouch in their dens,
    or lie in wait in their covert? . . .

Is it by your wisdom that the hawk soars,
    and spreads its wings toward the south?[65]

At first, it sounds as if the Lord is bullying Job into submission, but the text asks us to hear these words more humorously, more ironically. As Lindsay Wilson notes, "A delicate balance has to be maintained, as Yahweh seeks to redirect Job's energies powerfully yet playfully. If Yahweh is too harsh, he would appear to endorse the views of the friends; if Yahweh is too weak, then Job will not hear what needs to be said."[66] He is also shifting Job's attention from the narrowly reciprocal face-to-face exchange he had been hoping for and moving him towards to a decentered participation in God's joyously great economy.

Where were you when I laid the foundation of the earth?
    Tell me, if you have understanding.
Who determined its measurements—surely you know!
    Or who stretched the line upon it?

65. Job 38:2, 31, 39–40; 39:26 NRSV.
66. Wilson, Job, 181.

On what were its bases sunk,
    or who laid its cornerstone
when the morning stars sang together
    and all the heavenly beings shouted for joy?[67]

Astonishingly, God's speech reveals not just divine power, but a massive attentiveness to creation. God exhaustively notices and delights in *everything*. Ostriches burying their eggs. Eagles feeding their young. Lions coming out at sunset. Nebulae. Sea monsters. There are almost no references to human action in this divine speech. In contrast with our often anthropocentric exclusivity, God's attention economy, it becomes clear, leaves nothing out.

Hearing all this, Job puts his hand over his mouth. It looks near the end of the speech as if Job has been so thoroughly decentered in creation that there is no room for any further action from him. It looks as if he will sit naked, scraping himself, with his hand over his mouth, to the end of his days. Eventually, as the Lord narrates more and more the doings of the Great Economy, Job experiences a profounder change than mere muteness. He confesses that his erstwhile demand that God enter into dialogue with him face to face has been fully satisfied. "Both God's appearance and God's words have met Job's needs, and now enable him to move on."[68]

I know that you can do all things,
    and that no purpose of yours can be thwarted.
"Who is this that hides counsel without knowledge?"
Therefore I have uttered what I did not understand,
    things too wonderful for me, which I did not know.
"Hear, and I will speak;
    I will question you, and you declare to me."
I had heard of you by the hearing of the ear,
    but now my eye sees you;
therefore I despise myself,
    and repent in dust and ashes.[69]

As Wilson notes, Job is repenting not *in* the dust and ashes, but *from* them. The commentator notes that the Hebrew phrasing here indicates an alteration of one's plans based on new information. "In other words, Job is now ready to resume normal relationships in society, the very thing he proceeds to do in the following verses."[70] What has changed for Job is not

---

67. Job 38:4–7 NRSV.
68. Wilson, *Job*, 204.
69. Job 42:2–6 NRSV.
70. Wilson, *Job*, 206–7.

a sudden awareness of his own sinfulness—indeed the Lord will soon tell Job's friends that Job has been speaking accurately about his past moral actions—but a new skepticism for the need to continue in grand isolation from society as a lonely sufferer.[71]

But then comes another surprising word, that the Lord has work for Job to do in community. Job is asked first to pray for his friends, who had been for so many days his enemies. This is an invitation to participation in the life and work of community-in-creation before God. Through his priestly mediation, the friends are pardoned for speaking so negligently. Then God restores the fortunes of Job. And finally, Job's community comes to a banquet bringing him gifts. In other words, when Job prays for his friends, he receives gifts—not from the friends, but from his community. The gifts are not payment for his rectitude. But there is great import in the economics here portrayed: people who had been Job's beneficiaries now become his benefactors. Instead of the towering philanthropist, the hyper-attentive moralist, Job finds himself the humbled enjoyer of mutuality and circulation.

A FRESH FORM OF SPIRITUAL CAPITAL

This chapter has used an ancient dialogue to dramatize the limits of dialogue, especially as a way of approaching reality and as a way of approaching organizational life. As we make our way through Job, it sounds at first as if there has been an interpersonal breakdown between Job and God, and between Job and his friends—a breakdown that can only be corrected by the restoration of a tightly reciprocal dialogue: *I have given you this; now you must give me that.* But the actual breakdown, the actual disruption, pertains to a piece of misused moral technology: the retributionist principle. The book of Job does not wholly subvert that principle—it matters at the end that Job is a righteous person who speaks of himself accurately—but the book does put retributionism into question as a one-tool-fixes-everything approach to life.

Along with the change in equipment, comes a change in communication. Instead of relying solely on face-to-face conversation, and the hoped-for exchange of interiorities and intentions, the characters of the book are welcomed into a multidirectional mutuality. Dialogue is not wholly displaced. What is displaced is a limited conception and practice of dialogue. The gift that comes with conversation need not be a one-on-one soul-to-soul connection. There can still be conversational exchange; Job prays *for* his friends, after all, and receives gifts *from* his community. The spiritual

71. Wilson, *Job*, 206–7.

capital here, though, does not arrive with a tightly reciprocal exchange, but with a generously mutual circulation. Job gives prayer to God on behalf of his friends and receives gifts from his friends and neighbors. This is not, *I give you this, so you give me that*; this is, *I give him that, and she gives them those, and they give me this.* John Barclay sums the giving-and-receiving dynamic this way: "what I give may not be matched by a return gift from the recipient but by a return from elsewhere in the community: as gifts circulate among us, everyone is constantly in the process of both giving and receiving."[72]

Another of the gifts that circulates in workplace community comes under the rubric of inspiration or motivation, a gift often moved by means of inspirational storytelling—to whose uncanny gambits we turn in the next chapter.

72. Quoted in Sampson, *The Promise of Social Enterprise*, 165.

4

The Limits of Epiphany

"YOU'RE UP NEXT," SHE says. I can barely hear her over the hullabaloo, but I nod quickly, hiding my disconcertment. My students and I are field-researching the job-training organization Cara on Desplaines Avenue on a cold morning in Chicago. The current speaker stands in a sacrosanct space at the center of concentric rows of chairs, where many others have stood since 2002 when Cara's Motivations ritual began. Bill Murray did a bit here. Senator Dick Durbin and Mayors Rahm Emanuel and Lori Lightfoot have made appearances. Mostly, though, it's been the luminously ordinary Cara participants, who have dug deep, as they say in the program, and passed the motivation. As Cara's website puts it, "Each morning, the circle holds a sacred place to be vulnerable and surprised by where you might find your dose of inspiration."[1] Robert White, a leader at Cara, described the ritual during our interview:

> Perhaps the most beautiful part about the practice is that it's an egalitarian space, where we're all peers. So whether you're a participant or a staff member or a guest, entering into that space requires that, if somebody taps you on the shoulder—of course, if we have a guest [who] outright refuses, then we're not going to force somebody to do something that they're not prepared to do . . . But the rules are that if you get tapped on the shoulder, you go in no matter who you are, so there's no—the Chief Program

1. "All About Motivations at Cara," Cara.

Officer, me, I can't be too cool to go in the circle, I can't be too
good for it, I can't be any better than anybody else in the room,
and we're sharing of our own experiences.[2]

But somehow, even though I'd transcribed Robert's words as qualitative research data in my notes, I hadn't seen the spotlight wending its way
through the crowd to *me*.

A woman had started things off earlier that morning, bursting into
the inner ring of people, giving everyone high-fives. The rest of us were
standing or sitting in the outer rings of chairs in the Cara Great Room. We
watched, a little blearily, as she ran around the circle clockwise and then
counterclockwise, shouting the ritualized greeting: "Good morning, Cara,
Cleanslate, and guests!" It's a liturgy, a call-and-response exchange that runs
through thirty minutes of storytelling and singing. Each speaker runs the
same circle twice, takes the stage, and responds to the prompt for the day—
which that morning happened to be something like, "Tell us a goal you have
set and what you're doing to achieve it." The tales arrived at every scale of
import. A woman told about trying to slip free of homelessness. A man told
about trying to make his bed every morning. The hardest thing about the
ritual, at least for me, is that after each story, the teller has to sing a song. I
haven't felt stage fright for a long time. But the last time I sang in public was
a mercifully forgettable solo in a high school musical.

Ask not for whom the mic comes; it comes for you. And when it does,
I make my way to the inner ring, meet the expectant gazes, and launch a
story about my most recent New Year's resolution. My doctor told me, I
explained, that I needed to lose seventeen pounds. How was I going to do
that? My daughter gave me the idea of making a habit chart, which I check
off at the end of the day, and so far, I say with a rise in inflection to indicate
the arrival of a revelation, I've lost nine pounds. The story's not *quite* ready
for the TED Talk circuit, but the crowd cheers the feat with generous enthu-
siasm. They join me in singing two lines of "If You're Happy and You Know
It, Clap Your Hands." I was, I did, and they clapped.

REGULATORY MECHANISMS IN
THE AFFECT ECONOMY

Speaking in a space like Motivations can feel good—if you follow the rules.
And the rules are enforced, so to speak, by what the crowd claps for, what
the faces light up for. You can break the rules, of course, but you'll kill the

---

2. White, interview by author, January 23, 2019.

vibe. Who wants to do that? Motivations didn't come up with these norms. They guide inspirational speaking in every corner of today's mainstream affective economy, and they have their affective economists—people like Simon Sinek, Donald Miller, and Seth Godin, who constantly adjust the "interest rates" of today's messaging:

Rule 1: Start and end with an idea: I had to speak, I quickly figured out, as if the overwhelm of life could be managed by the power of a good idea—the sort of thing Simon Sinek might sum up by saying, "start with Why."[3] The Motivations ritual does what Sinek envisions in every professional setting, as it "becomes the vessel through which a person with a clear purpose, cause or belief can speak to the outside world. But for a megaphone to work, clarity must come first. Without a clear message, what will you amplify?"[4] Whatever else I had when I took that microphone, I had to get my story down to its leanest expression. Get your idea clear, get it clearly into language, and the crowd will be inspired.

Rule 2: Start as hero, end as mentor: My story had to start with a self in a predicament. As another affective technician, Donald Miller, would say, the most resonant stories of our time work this way:

A Character
Has a Problem
And Meets a Guide
Who Gives Them a Plan
And Calls them to Action
That Helps Them Avoid Failure
And Ends in a Success.[5]

Miller's diagramming of the monomyth helps explain why I felt like I had to start with hearing bad news from my doctor, then move to a Guide (my daughter Allie) with a Plan (that Pinterest chart), and mark out the path to success (the loss of pounds on the way to the Celestial City of weight loss). Miller would suggest that, although my tale was okay, it would be better if I myself were not the hero. The people out there clapping and smiling, he would say, "don't generally care about your story; they care about their own."[6] Every good story needs "mentors, mystical characters that help us

---

3. Sinek, *Start with Why*, 7.

4. This particular account of persuasive narrative and inspirational affect has roots in a diffuse array of philosophical, sociological, and rhetorical theories. MacIntyre, *After Virtue*; Fisher, *Human Communication as Narration*.

5. Miller, *Building a Story Brand*, 29–37.

6. Miller, *Building a Story Brand*, ix.

along the way."[7] I could be a guide for the folks at Cara. Let the inspiration transfusion begin.

Rule 3: Show the world made a little better. Read Seth Godin's books, and you'll see him staring owlishly at his clients, pondering their bemusing psychologies, until their inner story comes clear, and the world becomes improvable. "And if you're having trouble making your contribution, realize your challenge is a story you are marketing to yourself. It is the marketing we do for ourselves, to ourselves, by ourselves, the story we tell ourselves, that can change everything."[8] Like Sinek, Godin assumes that ideas have priority over behavior, and like Miller, he assumes the privileged starting point of the individual protagonist. But he traces one more circuit in the Motivations economy: the world has been made one way; it can be remade another through imaginative and innovative action.

For me, making a speech and singing a song on that February morning was hard. But keeping those rules was easy. I'd seen them reinforced in movie representations of Alcoholics Anonymous and half-time locker-rooms. I'd heard them performed on the Moth Radio Hour on public radio Saturday afternoons and then in sermon illustrations on Sunday morning. The rules clarify just about every speakerly choice. What kind of eye contact should you keep? Well, you have to speak from your inmost self—that's where the story starts—so don't let your gaze go dead. You have to be a mentor, so move close to your audience, if you can. But give them room, too. Don't get all vampire on them, ogling their souls. And speak in an accessible, personable tone of voice that suggests it's just you and each person, a twosome in a crowd. Vary your pitches so you have a wide range of pathos, both for the humorously prosaic details and the last piercing insight. Make those choices, and good feelings follow as morning does the night.

As I think back over my research data, I recognize these norms at work among the organizational leaders I spoke with. My interviewees, organizational leaders in dozens of small organizations, do this "affective labor" all the time: inspiring their investors, motivating their workers, building donor excitement, assuring stakeholders that the world is getting a little better.[9] Tim Brand is a skilled narrator of his own spiritual awakening on August 11, 2005, the "Inspiration Day" when he woke up to his calling to serve the people of Haiti. His spiritual realization and its resultant "holy discontent" led eventually to founding Many Hands for

7. Miller, *Building a Story Brand*, 74.
8. Godin, *This is Marketing*, 252.
9. Hardt, "Affective Labor," 89–100.

Haiti, a faith-based non-governmental development organization in the central plains region of Haiti.[10]

Although an inspirational story like this can be told quickly and concisely, some of my research subjects had their questions about the value of this brevity, especially when it came to working with others in community.[11] As powerful a kickstarter for one's own engagements as this kind of inspiration can be, ginning up motivation day after day, person after person, can be tiring.[12] One of my research subjects, a social entrepreneur and real estate developer in West Baltimore, Bree Jones, conducted her second interview with me in the middle of a personal spiritual retreat where she was taking time to contemplate what she called her hero's journey.

> I actually try to shy away from this notion that we need heroes ... at the same time I realize that ... as much as I'm leaning into this collectiveness, I have really been the person who's pushing this forward.[13]

The hero's journey was actually a space-holder—until the collective narrative could get going. Eventually, the change her organization sought in the neighborhoods of Baltimore had to be a collective project. "I'm excited," she said, "to get to the place where it no longer relies on just my energy."[14]

Bree has me thinking about the limits of the inspirational story as a mode of spiritual capital. She is not alone. Other leaders I spoke with put

10. Brand, *Transforming Together*, 1.

11. I met Thomas Hampton at SOCAP, a conference for social impact investors, and he underwent some training there to learn to tell his inspirational story in twenty seconds. He had his doubts. "So, from a utilitarian perspective, I have no doubt that it's a good strategy. It makes a lot of sense to me, actually. But just from how I live and want my life to go and the patterns—speaking of spiritual practices, I guess—I just want to follow where conversations go. If I get an investor, I want to ask the investor ... what are they working on? Why are they giving their money to something? That's not a great way to raise money, probably, but I don't care that much. I want to get to know people and know what they care about ... and even how they are as a person." Hampton, interview by author, October 23, 2019.

12. Condit got me thinking about the limits of this optimism in her book-length study of public anger, which itself has an optimistic dynamic. Despite her critique of *public* anger, she concedes it can be individually vital. "Our anger ... motivates us to act, but the action needed is not necessarily the broad sharing of our anger as it comes raging up in us, formed as it is by the essentializing and binarizing forces of language in interaction with orientations to attack, and resistant as it is to novel cognition." Condit, *Angry Public Rhetorics*, 8. What is needed can be only inadequately summarized here: she recommends a broadening of the range of feelings publics rely on. (See her discussion in Chapter 7 of *Angry Public Rhetorics*.)

13. Mattson, "Telling the Neighborhood Story—Bree Jones."

14. Jones, interview by author, December 15, 2020.

in question the sustainability of the inspiration circuit. As CEO of the job-training and socially entrepreneurial organization, New Moms, Laura Zumdahl knows as many hopeful stories as anybody I've ever met. But she also has tales to tell about every "sexy new thing" as donors and investors "shift 'strategic priorities' every few years (often after pausing funding for a year or more to 'evaluate our work and determine how to strategically focus on particular issue areas'), which doesn't really move the needle on any new or developing thing."[15] Laura has seen this cycle of fascination followed by boredom recur often over the past two decades. "Funding housing for people experiencing homelessness is a big priority . . . until it's not and then it's funding workforce development . . . and then it's not . . . and now it's social enterprise . . . until it's not and we're back to housing being important again."[16] The way she puts this recalls a passage from the wisdom literature of the Old Testament:

> The wind blows to the south,
>   and goes around to the north;
> round and round goes the wind,
>   and on its circuits the wind returns.
> All streams run to the sea,
>   but the sea is not full;
> to the place where the streams flow,
>   there they continue to flow;
> All things are wearisome;
>   more than one can express.[17]

Laura sounds, in other words, like Qoheleth, the Solomonic literary figure at the heart of the book of Ecclesiastes.

So does Corey Kohn of DOJO4, sometimes. I remember once, in an incidental conversation, hearing her tell her own Ecclesiastes story. She and her team get a good idea for some way to bring change in the world: a new brand expression, an innovative product, a novel way to manage tasks, a new platform for connecting with clients. Everybody's energized by the change. For a few weeks, the mood of the office is inspired, motivated, engaged. But then, the newness wears off. A slump settles into the organizational posture. Corey realizes, with a little chagrin, and a lot of tiredness, that somehow, someway, they need to innovate all over again—not because the world needs that particular change exactly, but because organizational

15. Zumdahl, email message to author, August 10, 2020.
16. Zumdahl, email message to author, August 10, 2020.
17. Ecclesiastes 1:6–8a NRSV.

productivity seems to rely on pushing the boulder of innovation back up the mountain one more time.

Chasing or pushing the latest bright and shiny object up the mountain is, of course, what humans have always done. There's nothing new under the sun, and if something new could show up, nobody could focus on it for long.

> What has been is what will be,
>   and what has been done is what will be done;
>   there is nothing new under the sun.
> Is there a thing of which it is said,
>   "See, this is new"?
> It has already been,
>   in the ages before us.
> The people of long ago are not remembered,
>   nor will there be any remembrance
> of people yet to come
>   by those who come after them.[18]

These words from Ecclesiastes raise dark questions about what keeps humans getting up every morning and going to work—or what keeps organizational leaders designing new ideas for their teams.

The book opens with a wry and earthy prologue insisting that every single thing humans do turns out to be "stinking hot air"—which is Cal Seerveld's rendering of the vital Hebrew word *hevel*. This term usually gets translated in Ecclesiastes as "vanity," as in the familiar phrase, "vanity of vanities." But Seerveld's rendering reveals the gaseous, foul, windy, and fleeting semantics of *hevel*. "It's all just a big fart!" Then comes the devastating question, "What's a person got left after all his or her hard work? / a person who does their damned best on this earth—what's left?!"[19]

Qoheleth then opens his anti-motivational oration. Speeches are not unusual in the wisdom books: the book of Proverbs fills its first nine chapters, and Job nearly all its chapters, with orations.[20] But across all the literary styles of Ecclesiastes—poems, rhetorical questions, quotations, parables, oracles, blessings, and commands—Craig Bartholomew traces "the royal testament or fictional autobiography cast in a frame narrative" that counters just about every TED Talk ever given.[21]

---

18. Ecclesiastes 1:9–11 NRSV.

19. Seerveld, "Ecclesiastes."

20. Mackie and Collins, "Wisdom Series: Proverbs."

21. Bartholomew, *Ecclesiastes*, 74. Bartholomew is my source for the different literary styles in the book. See especially 61–63.

Qohleth first identifies himself to his audience of skeptics: "Look, I'm a philosopher."[22] In Seerveld's translation, this is a conventional self-identifier; the teacher is saying he's a cultural leader and storyteller, who, like other rabbis or imams, will share a "Once upon a time" story formulation about his experiment to discern what life and work are for.[23] "And I thought to myself, how about looking into things to find out by wisdom what the sense is to all that's being done under the heavens."[24] He develops a life experiment:

> I made great works; I built houses and planted vineyards for myself; I made myself gardens and parks, and planted in them all kinds of fruit trees. I made myself pools from which to water the forest of growing trees. I bought male and female slaves, and had slaves who were born in my house; I also had great possessions of herds and flocks, more than any who had been before me in Jerusalem. I also gathered silver and gold and the treasure of kings and of the provinces.[25]

Not only does he become a developer and an agronomist, taking up project after ambitious project, he also enjoys the good things of life: sex, food, wine, and the rest that comes after a hard day's work. He even delves into folly, refusing to take himself too seriously: "I was determined to be familiar not only with what makes sense and is valuable but also to know intimately all kinds of mad foolishness and outright stupidity."[26] But the end of all his enterprise and careful observation leads to the conclusion that all this aspiration, all this effort, all this growth in understanding proves only "that wisdom too is a sometime thing" and the "pitiable fact" that "the philosopher like his fellow fool ends up dead!"[27] Human enterprise, he suggests, is on a highway to *hevel*.

Qoheleth's insights make inspirational speech sound uncanny, at least to me. My own Motivations speech, now that I look back on it, reminds me of a computer-generated image: life-like but a little creepy.[28] There I was, a middle-class, comfortably employed, house-owning, super-insulated, slightly doughy, very pasty guy, telling all these kindly people, against whom every structure of inequity has been lodged for four-hundred-plus years, that they can do what they put their minds to.

22. Seerveld, "Ecclesiastes."

23. Seerveld, email message to author, September 27, 2011.

24. Seerveld, "Ecclesiastes."

25. Ecclesiastes 2:4–8a NRSV.

26. Seerveld, "Ecclesiastes."

27. Seerveld, "Ecclesiastes."

28. Mori, "The Uncanny Valley," 33–35.

But then, come to think of it, even an inspired communicator like Bree raises questions about individual inspiration in relation to collective change. And Laura, still further down the road of organizational leadership, knows all too well the uncanny optimism of thinking that this donor, this invest-ment, will bring the needed change in the world. The inspirational story has short-term power, admittedly, especially with the suits downtown, the wealthy senior citizens, the monied churchgoers. But the stories of orga-nizational leaders I'm about to share raise a further question: What if the story you are trying to activate in an organization or a neighborhood doesn't begin with the interior life, the innovative ideas, of the individual hero, seeking to mold the world to some already specified goal? Is there an affect economy more comprehensive than the circuits set by affect technicians like Sinek, Miller, and Godin? Is there an economy of greater affection, one that comprises all the actual conditions of human life?

THE LIMITS OF INSPIRATION

Of all the stories I scribbled down in my ninety-eight-cent composition notebooks, none tracks more closely with the mainstream affect economy than does the epiphanic narrative that Tiffany Hinton tells leading up to her social enterprises Wild Mamas and Movement Apparatus. When Tiff was a teenager, she found herself ensnared in a fundamentalist cult. The group arranged a marriage for her, and she eventually became the mother of two. But after her first child came along, she began to have inklings that all was not well with this group. She began to feel restless in a community that had originally promised stability. Things worsened to such a degree that, after the birth of her second child, she experienced an awakening, but away from organized faith. She now describes her experience of this cult with a figure of sexual violence: "I think the way that I describe that experience was that I felt like I had been spiritually raped."[29] At age twenty-five, she divorced her husband, left the membership, and set off on her own heroic journey determined to make the world better than she'd been found by it.

Today, she practices an eclectic and determined spirituality that entails rigorous practice. Each morning, she rises at 2:30 and meditates, journals, and cares for her children. "I found that early morning when it's quiet and dark and you know, the moon is out, that it's a time that really grounds me and allows me to come into my own spiritual sacred space."[30] Her mention of the moon is deliberate: having repudiated the Bible and other sources of

29. Hinton, interview by author, March 31, 2019.
30. Hinton, interview by author, March 31, 2019.

Christian teaching, she now draws on the wisdom resources of indigenous spirituality, especially tracing to her Celtic and African roots.

> And so I also tend to encourage others to be mindful of the seasons and the rhythms of the earth and nature and work to align themselves to that. Because obviously we're products of the universe and Earth and nature, and the more we can get into those rhythms, the more we can tap into the universal life force and energy that exists. I do believe that there's another spiritual realm, there's an energetic, a spiritual realm we can't see, but is very much a part of our day-to-day life.[31]

Her post-secular conversion experience has entailed not just a personal repudiation of the church; it has also led to the development of two business consultancies aimed towards pro-social ends. Her main company, Movement Apparatus, is a consulting company that inhabits what social entrepreneurs like to call the "values space," especially by assisting socially minded organizations to extend their political impact and grow their movements. Her ancillary company, Wild Mamas, supports woman-owned businesses "geared towards supporting mamas, mothers, to find, step into, and own their purpose and power."[32] She notes that she is not stuck in the trauma she has experienced but nonetheless draws on it in her work.

> A lot of people that I work with and coach—they happen to be other women, especially other mamas like myself—and so I tend to then kind of coach from that place of them putting themselves first, which I believe is deeply spiritual, you know, being connected to yourself and your truth and who you are as a person and a human being. And so I tend to coach from that place of self-care and self-love but also from figuring out your own vision, values, and purposes—which I feel for me, all of that is spiritual.[33]

Tiff conveys an idealist conviction that everything begins with the location of action within the inspired and courageous individual.

But Tiff also has ambivalence about the affect economy of uncanny optimism, especially as it gets expressed in White and privileged gatherings. She believes that personal inspiration can circulate and can change the world. She's not so sure that everyone's inspiration, however, is equally efficacious. Sometimes the mainstream affect economy strikes her as too—White.

31. Hinton, interview by author, March 31, 2019.
32. Hinton, interview by author, March 31, 2019.
33. Hinton, interview by author, March 31, 2019.

I met Tiff for the first time at a social business conference, a gathering of some two hundred practitioners dedicated to authentic sharing and inspirational speaking. We were asked to observe collective meditative practices—keep both feet on the floor, breathe from your center, practice radical openness, etc.—and to talk to our neighbors, sharing closely personal elements from our lives. Because I was at the conference as a participant observer, I took furious notes, alternating my scribbling with quick glances around the room. I remember seeing Tiff on the periphery, carrying her infant son wrapped in a baby sling and bouncing and swaying gently, coaxing her baby to rest, despite the voices filling the space.

Once, during a question-and-answer time, she raised her hand for one of the presenters to bring her a mic in order to ask a question about race in the sector. As one of the few people of color in the gathering—she had counted three African Americans, she told me—she was herself a sign that all was not as well as the inspirational stories onstage might indicate. Her standpoint as a Black woman looking on from the back of the auditorium, enabled her to see what was missing onstage and in the room. "I felt that most of the people on that stage were people who were running extremely large organizations that sought investor funding and whatever. So, I felt like, yes, they're kind of trying to push this social way, but their investment and their funding strategy is still the same as everybody else's" in the business world.[34] Hinton found herself thinking of other social innovators not mentioned at this conference, not represented on the stage or seated in the expensively ticketed seats—and yet just as absorbed in the work of integrating business with social justice. The people whose faces came to mind would probably not describe themselves as "social entrepreneurs," she explained. That term connotes a privilege sometimes unknown to minority practitioners at the intersection of business and justice.

> I feel like there's a lot of young people like me who are kind of globally minded. We're diverse and mixed and we're just living a different kind of life and we value people, we value our health and well-being and the health and well-being of others, and we care, we care about our communities and care about our people. And so we're doing a lot of this work, but we're not in those spaces having those kinds of conversations.[35]

Perhaps because of my White-guy standpoint, I found the speakers at the conference to be as genuine as any I've ever heard speak. I was impressed by their willingness to talk about failures they've endured. I liked

34. Hinton, interview by author, March 31, 2019.
35. Hinton, interview by author, March 31, 2019.

the dabbling in spiritual practice they led us through collectively. I found their inspirational speaking moving. But Tiff hinted at stories of people *not* represented at the conference, people whom she felt were the true "cultural shapeshifters and movers" who "are going to change the world."[36] Tiff can tell the conventional inspiration story when she wants to. At the same time, her comments and concerns were among my first indicators in this organizational research that the inspirational story hooked into a rather exclusivist affect economy.

I interviewed someone later, Jon Berbaum of Highland Solutions, whom I discovered to be a friend of Tiff's. He's something of a modern-day Qoheleth, at least in the way he distrusts what he calls the "hand-waving around conscious capitalism," which is actually "perpetuating a structure that is in some ways, many ways, unjust or distasteful by tacking on good stuff."[37] Berbaum describes this deleterious altruism this way:

> There's this world-changing rhetoric that has turned ugly and evil, and yet there's still all these thousands of people working at those organizations, trying to salvage it or barely going along pretending nothing's wrong or something. But the "we're gonna change the world and it's gonna be so awesome" optimism and naivete that at scale has turned into this, at best, deeply compromised reality, is definitely on my mind.[38]

Jon helps me notice that Tiff's stories have some contradictions. Despite her pessimism about White, corporatized individualism, she has her own pronounced individualist and idealist tendencies: she approaches life with an uber-positivity and sidesteps the negativity of the mainstream news. She talks about herself in frankly heroic and transformationalist terms. She appears to see herself as a world-changer by the sheer power of will and thought.

But perhaps in this tension between critique and optimism, she is like Qoheleth. Commentators have spent a lot of ink trying to reconcile the many contradictions of this book. If he thinks life is a big, gaseous lot of nothing, then how can he recommend that people enjoy food and work and life with their spouse? These passages are often referred to as *carpe diem* passages, saying things like, "There is nothing better for mortals than to eat and drink, and find enjoyment in their toil."[39] Are these passages resiliently optimistic, or are they cynically resigned? Seerveld's translation resolves this

---

36. Hinton, interview by author, March 31, 2019.

37. Berbaum, interview by author, May 2, 2019.

38. Berbaum, interview by author, May 2, 2019.

39. Ecclesiastes 2:24 NRSV.

question by casting the characters of the book in a busily garrulous community dialogue—a multi-logue that sounds like Tiff's global community of shape-shifters. Seerveld renders them as shifting constantly from prosaic maxims to agonizing observations to deeply steadying wisdom—and, in the course of the overall conversation, acknowledging the brutalities and the possibilities of the human condition.[40] Qoheleth thus comes off as a speechmaker whose narratives are constantly poked at and agreed with and countered by other voices, giving the text the feel of an unruly conference where attenders are perpetually arguing, affirming, misunderstanding, challenging, and counter-stating the findings of the keynote speaker. Maybe Tiff feels free to try out her ideas in so many directions because she knows that hers is hardly the only voice.

Seerveld's polyphonous translation is, admittedly, venturesome; but he is surely right to see that behind the interactions of the book is a somewhat unreliable narrator, to use Wayne Booth's handy terminology, making a larger point than either optimism or pessimism can account for—that we are all unavoidably involved in an enfolding economy that we cannot extricate ourselves from.[41]

Let me switch to another case study, this one about a commercial banker, Charlie Branda, living in the Sedgwick neighborhood of Chicago, who one day heard a gunshot outside her home. She and her children soon learned that a man, a Black man as it happened, had been gunned down just across from their home on one of the closely segregated streets in Chicago, wealthy Whites on one side of the street and low-income housing, often peopled with Black folk, on the other. She stood in her home feeling forlorn, discomfited, restless, uncertain where (as she put it) to take a casserole with condolences. *We have to know each other*, she thought. And then, because she is not the sort of person to waste an epiphany, she decided to launch a social enterprise called Art on Sedgwick that would seek to have neighbors making things together. Although Charlie knew next to nothing about art, she knew something about community infrastructure from her years as a community banker. She started inviting citizens from both sides of the Sedgwick Avenue into a studio space to do paint-and-sip or steppin' dance instruction. Some of her organization's most remarkable work has been with children from widely different schools in the neighborhood, teaching them how to collaborate in artistic creation. Charlie's story is compelling enough to draw attention from major news networks and to

---

40. Seerveld, "Ecclesiastes."
41. Booth, *The Rhetoric of Fiction*, 158.

garner a TEDx Talk.[42] She has become not only a company president, but a community leader as well.

I have taken students to visit Art on Sedgwick numerous times, sometimes just to get acquainted with the neighborhood, sometimes to study the story Charlie tells. One of my rhetoric classes spent a semester developing multiple potential versions of Charlie's story as a way to game out a TED-Talk-styled presentation. She strikes me both as someone keenly aware of the affect economy that dominates contemporary society and someone who pushes back on it. She seems to embrace the idealism of uncanny optimism: she earnestly believes that what needs to change in her neighborhood is the ideas neighbors have in their heads about each other. If she can just create encounters, those ideas will change—and so will her neighborhood. But although Charlie's story has a heroic quality to it, grounding the locus (as inspirational stories so often must today) in her own realization of an insight, she is remarkably unconcerned about herself as an essential part of what is going on in her neighborhood.

She likes to tell about how her son one day warned her that if she kept up her work, one of the local drug dealers would start to feel territorial and end up shooting her. Charlie thought about this for a while.

> I didn't think that that would really happen. But I was trying to understand from my son's perspective, okay, he's probably really afraid of that. And then I tried to imagine—there's never been a White person shot in my neighborhood, so I don't feel like it's a very big danger. But then I was like, somebody could get mad at me, because if I'm trying to create all this beauty—basically, I feel like beauty can counteract bad stuff because if there's beauty there, people aren't going to want to sell drugs there. If there's beauty there, drug dealers aren't going to feel comfortable there. So, I could see maybe they would get mad. Like, I made friends with that idea. What if somebody came up to me, pulled out a gun, shot me right in the face, and I died? Would I be okay with that?[43]

As with Tiff, Charlie shows a remarkable gift for telling a compelling hero story. But her reflections point beyond the confines of that story to a larger way of being. She approaches her life and work, for instance, with a kind of detachment about her own survival. She sees Art on Sedgwick as less about what she is capable of and more about what can be set loose in the Sedgwick neighborhood.

42. Branda, "Art Helps Diverse Neighbors."
43. Branda, interview by author, June 28, 2019.

Because Charlie's story begins with the death of a neighbor, she often evinces a feel for the mortality that reminds me of Qoheleth. He asks the bitter questions the rest of us would rather avert our gaze from: "How can the wise die just like fools?"[44] He names the predicament that is our most widely shared condition:

> For the fate of humans and the fate of animals is the same; as one dies, so dies the other. They all have the same breath, and humans have no advantage over the animals; for all is vanity. All go to one place; all are from the dust, and all turn to dust again. Who knows whether the human spirit goes upward and the spirit of animals goes downward to the earth?[45]

> I thought the dead, who have already died, more fortunate than the living, who are still alive.[46]

> It is better to go to the house of mourning than to go to the house of feasting; for this is the end of everyone, and the living will take it to heart.[47]

In these passages, there is something to offend everyone, from the pious person concerned to defend the doctrine of resurrection to the postsecular activist determined that the world must be perfectible. But what Qoheleth's irreverence does not say, Ellen Davis warns, should not obscure what he *does* say about human life. He is not trying to teach about the mortality or immortality of the soul like the Greeks of his time. But he is offering "the very important message . . . . namely, that human beings inescapably share the fate of all the creatures."[48] As Davis points out, Qoheleth sees in the closeness of death a binding together of people with places and things in vital ways. We are immanent to each other. We are immanent to animals. We are immanent to the soil we tread. It's not an optimistic story, but it is an ultimately encompassing economy.

Here's a third and final story for this chapter's discussion of inspirational storytelling that pushes back on the affect economy of our time.

Corey Kohn and her partners were working at a company that was busy and successful. But they felt that the meaning had somehow drained out of it. "We had this crisis of conscience, if that's what you want to call it.

44. Ecclesiastes 2:16 NRSV.

45. Ecclesiastes 3:19 NRSV.

46. Ecclesiastes 4:2 NRSV.

47. Ecclesiastes 7:2 NRSV.

48. Davis, *Proverbs, Ecclesiastes, and the Song of Songs*, 186.

And we decided to fire everyone and start a new business."[49] The company-wide firing was a self-admittedly theatrical move: they invited everyone to rejoin the organization, but as a socially aspirational company doing meaningful work. DOJO4 is today a computer software company that pursues business, but not as usual. Corey's awakening story helps make sense of their unconventional choices to be a "member-owned tech cooperative," committed to being a zebra (that is, a colorful company, but a real one) in a world of entrepreneurial unicorns (that is, wildly successful but often fictive organizations).[50] As a Buddhist, Corey is wholly conversant in contemplative practice and writes about it articulately on her company blog, and this epiphanic story of personal and collective conscience-strickenness enacts the good unconventionality and reliable iconoclasm of her company. It also moves in the circuits of the idealist, heroic, and constructivist narratives of the contemporary affect economy. Perhaps software designers with a background in the arts like Corey are especially amenable to the notion that just about anything can be redesigned for the better, if only you gather bold, innovative protagonists in a compelling storyline.

But Corey also pushes back on the uncanny optimism of the mainstream affect economy:

> I live in this place where it's really super left-leaning, very progressive. It's also incredibly wealthy. I was born here, and I can't afford to buy a house here. It's crazy. What's happened here? It's like, you never have someone over to lunch without asking them about their dietary restrictions. It's that kind of thing. Everyone does yoga. Also, everybody is White. Everyone is wealthy.[51]

That kind of progressivism often brings with it, notes Tara Isabella Burton, a spiritually informed perfectionism. "At its most effective, social justice culture creates a mythic narrative about the world we live in, filling the seeming chaos of history and its myriad injustices with an eschatological promise: that human beings can, should, and shall do better."[52] Corey's quickness to laugh at herself, not to mention her willingness to do the contaminated and bourgeois thing of running a for-profit company, suggests that she's suspicious of perfectionism. She delights to tell how at first her social enterprise insisted on working with aspirational

---

49. Kohn, interview by author, May 20, 2019.

50. "DOJO4," DOJO4.

51. Kohn, interview by author, May 20, 2019.

52. Burton, *Strange Rites,* 178.

(or, as she put it "righteous") companies, but came to see this as an irresponsible exclusivity.

Corey's willingness to plunge right into a sector that has been historically deeply committed to sexism, racism, and devastating harms to our planet reminds me of Qoheleth's own anti-perfectionism, even his counterintuitive pity for the oppressor. "On the side of their oppressors there was power—with no one to comfort them."[53] He is not eliding the difference between victims and perpetrators: that such injustice exists at all makes him wish never to have been born. But he also realizes that, as Davis notes, "It is not enough to tell the oppressor to stop oppressing; in most cases, oppression does not represent a conscious choice. Rather a mistreatment of others is a way one has learned to survive in a sick family, a sick political system, a sick economy."[54] Qoheleth has a profound sense of the way that people's lives on the right and wrong sides of history are bound together in a fundamentally precarious condition: mortality.

I experienced Corey's own sense of that mortality in a collaborative project. For a few months in the late summer and fall of 2019, Corey and I worked together to launch a podcast called *Spiritual Capital*. It proved to be a challenging but joyous collaboration: challenging, because I was in Chicago and she in Boulder; joyous, because Corey brought to the collaboration the energy and even the hilarity that she brings to all her work. As we conducted video chat sessions, as we collaborated in online docs, as we chatted by phone, I saw evidence that her epiphanic story at DOJO4 had resulted in an integrality in her life and work. Once, while we were trying to solve a tech problem, Corey's daughter appeared in her mother's lap, peering into the screen like some gorgeous little being who had just swum up, keen, colorful, avid of life.

Later, Corey had to step back from the podcast. The demands of running a company and caring for her parents and her family and, oh, just all the other things made sense of her departure. I had enjoyed the lovely every-which-way-ness of our collaborative work. The collaboration felt like a kind of network hospitality, in which she and I enjoyed vibrant encounters with each other's vocations. I introduced her to students of mine who assisted in tech questions and editing processes; she introduced me to coworkers and family as well. But mostly what I learned from Corey, I think, is her sense of the rhythm she tries to keep in life, a cadence straight out of Qoheleth:

> For everything there is a season, and a time for every matter under heaven:
> a time to be born, and a time to die;

53. Ecclesiastes 4:1 NRSV.
54. Davis, *Proverbs, Ecclesiastes, and the Song of Songs,* 189–90.

a time to plant, and a time to pluck up what is planted;
a time to kill, and a time to heal;
a time to break down, and a time to build up;
a time to weep, and a time to laugh;
a time to mourn, and a time to dance;
a time to throw away stones, and a time to gather stones together.[55]

That last image, as commentator Ellen Davis notes, is a business meta-phor that Corey could appreciate: the stones are probably being used for accounting purposes. But in any case, Qoheleth is naming these "moments of life that more often than not are thrust upon us and likewise pass away, whether we wish it or not." Like those times when Corey has to, for reasons of personal integrity and family care, say no when her soul's habit is affirma-tion instead. But, not even a super competent soul is able to "determine the times for most of the important things in life, nor even choose 'the business . . . to be busy with' . . . for that is a gift from God."[56] Corey's cheerfulness is tempered by her awareness that the world is not entirely amenable to what we think, who we are, what we do. "I think that having a spiritual awaken-ing," she told me once, "or having a sense of a personal spiritual practice or anything like that can have a lot of good feelings involved, but often times what it awakens to is the inherent difficulty of life."[57]

The inspirational narrative that Tiff, Charlie, and Corey know how to tell is not difficult to learn, nor difficult to follow as a listener. But, as their ambivalence suggested, the form is not without its limits. All stories select some plot elements and leave others out. But so much is squeezed out of the inspirational narrative that it feels less like selection and more like subtraction—in particular the subtraction of stories that do not begin with the intentions of a solitary character; whose central crisis is not a problem resolvable by goodwill, savvy, and hard work; in which persons are integral but not central; and in which the needed capabilities are not to outwit or overcome, but rather to attune and release. In such cases, the organizational leader needs another sort of narrative, hooking into an even more comprehensive circuit of affective exchanges than we have seen so far in this chapter.

55. Ecclesiastes 3:1–5 NRSV.
56. Davis, *Proverbs, Ecclesiastes, and the Song of Songs*, 184.
57. Kohn, interview by author, May 20, 2019.

SEEKING ANOTHER ECONOMY OF AFFECT

For most of the book, Qoheleth's bitter storytelling refuses all inspiration and comfort, but two-thirds of the way through the book, the philosopher finally gives up on his project to encapsulate life and work. "All this I have tested by wisdom; I said, 'I will be wise,' but it was far from me. That which is, is far off, and deep, very deep; who can find it out?"[58] The book does not, however, counsel cynical sloth or despairing inaction. Qoheleth, in fact, counsels his community to generous undertakings in an unmanageable world. In a passage that repeatedly emphasizes what we cannot possibly know, he says,

> Send out your bread upon the waters,
>   for after many days you will get it back.
> Divide your means seven ways, or even eight,
>   for you do not know what disaster may happen on earth.[59]

There's an important difference between this call to entrepreneurial risk-taking and the risk-taking usually celebrated in today's affective economy. Entrepreneurship, after all, relies upon risk by the possibility of reward. Sure, you might lose; most entrepreneurships fail. Still, the opportunity to win makes the risk worthwhile. But here, as Davis points out, Qoheleth encourages risk without the prospect of reward. "The logic is staggering," she notes. "Not only should you give without certainty of repayment; you should give with the fair certainty of *not* being repaid."[60]

The book of Ecclesiastes concludes with an evocation of aging and death, as Qoheleth envisions his own gradual, painful loss of faculties. After calling young people to keep in mind their relationship to their Maker, the philosopher offers a series of metaphors of bodily decay, concluding with sorrowful anticipation of when "the silver cord is snapped, and the golden bowl is broken, and the pitcher is broken at the fountain, and the wheel broken at the cistern, and the dust returns to the earth as it was, and the breath returns to God who gave it. Vanity of vanities, says the Teacher; all is vanity."[61]

Needless to say, there isn't much room in motivational speaking today for talk about how one's body is going to gradually fall apart.[62] But the fact

---

58. Ecclesiastes 7:23–24 NRSV.

59. Ecclesiastes 11:1–2 NRSV.

60. Davis, *Proverbs, Ecclesiastes, and the Song of Songs*, 220.

61. Ecclesiastes 12:6–8 NRSV.

62. I did hear Tyler Etters, one of my interview subjects, reflect aloud on his own death in an almost Qoheleth-like fashion: "I was sitting on a train reading a book going

that death unites us all in a common mortality should perhaps be considered a more enlivening truth that it usually is. In any case, the book of Ecclesiastes helps to make apparent one of the problems with uncanny optimism—its inevitable affective narrowing. Wendell Berry has argued that the mark of a good economy is how much it comprehends.[63] But there are only so many feelings comprehended in the usual course of inspirational storytelling—feelings this chapter has rubricked as uncanny optimism. But what about feelings often excluded: sadness, lament, indignation, despair, overwhelm?

Those feelings don't sound particularly productive, perhaps. How do they comport with organizational leadership? Here, too, Qoheleth's dour testimony can be helpful, especially in connection with what his editor says about him at the end of the book. As commentator Peter Enns points out, what is most striking about the conclusion of Ecclesiastes is that the listening narrator affirms Qoheleth, calling him "a wise philosopher"—"And what's written here is right!"[64] For all the skepticism, for all the contradiction, for all the obsession with death, this philosopher is wise and worth considering. The editor does not try to eliminate what Qoheleth has said, nor does he find the teaching to contradict what faithfulness has always meant for followers of God's way. The book concludes by calling its readers in good Hebrew fashion to fear God and keep his commandments. As Enns points out, Qoheleth's terrible statements regarding injustice and suffering in human life actually provide strength and motivation for shared faithful action.[65]

Just as Job becomes a beneficiary after so many years of being a philanthropist, Qoheleth finds his instruction received and improved upon by the community where he does his work. The bread he has cast on the water—the sayings he has shared and the stories he has told—has come back to him in the affirmation of listening community. And the recipients of this teaching can both acknowledge the truth of his grim account of human life and yet affirm the need to walk reverently and faithfully. The frame story of the book addressed to a suffering and displaced people thus practices a complex acknowledgement, saying yes to Qoheleth's anti-inspirational insights without permitting that to be the only word. In the course of doing so, the book

to school, and I put the book down and look out the window and said, I'm going to die. And that's when I came to terms with my reality. I wasn't afraid, I wasn't worried, I wasn't anxious, it was just: I'm going to die. Great. That's awesome. Just realizing it as an absolute, I felt completely liberated, and ever since then I've just felt this lightness." Etters, interview by author, April 11, 2019.

63. Berry, "The Two Economies."

64. Seerveld, "Ecclesiastes."

65. Enns, *Ecclesiastes*, 110–16.

points to possibilities for a counter-narrative form. Such a counter-story need not be anti-heroic or anti-inspirational like Qoheleth's testimony but could be instead a completely different genre of story altogether. The next chapter workshops one fresh kind of storytelling in terms of the Neighborhood Story.

5

Telling Company Stories
That Start with Place

BREE JONES WILL TELL you that Old West Baltimore has good bones. The way she sees it, the historic character of the architecture, the proximity of public transport systems, and the deep cultural history of the people form the underlying foundation of a strong neighborhood

"I feel very fortunate that I learned early on not to pathologize Black people and Black spaces," she told me during a podcast interview, "despite the dominant teachings of race and space in America."[1] The real story here, she says, is not a story of failed citizenly motivation. It is a story of unjust policies in the housing industry. "When I see neighborhoods with boarded-up buildings, my first thought isn't 'Wow, who was the person who lived here who let their home deteriorate into this?' My first thought is, 'Wow, look at these decades and centuries of purposeful, intentional, and legislated disinvestment on a federal, state, and local level.'"[2]

When Bree first launched the social entrepreneurship Parity Homes, she found herself contending with a sometimes-exploitative real estate industry determined to appropriate a city block for gilt upscale homes and chic businesses that would push long-time locals out. But now, having established a presence in the region, Parity Homes has begun to do its

1. Mattson, "Telling the Neighborhood Story—Bree Jones."
2. Mattson, "Telling the Neighborhood Story—Bree Jones."

own development work in a neighbor-centric way. "We started Parity as a response to the gentrification and displacement we experienced in our hometown," Bree's website notes. "Now we're working to do development without displacement, and create ownership in the process."[3] Her organizational model involves recruiting people who commit to living in and caring for a single city block. By building cohorts, thirty citizens at a time, she adds social musculature to the good bones of these neighborhoods. DeAmon Harges once told me that economic capital not infrequently comes from social capital, and Bree seems to have learned much the same thing.[4] Her economic development work builds on people's doing the human thing of committing to care for each other: "A healthy neighborhood," she says, "is just one in which the residents and the neighborhoods care about one another and have a vested interest in one another's success and health."[5]

But there's a kind of spiritual capital at play here prior even to either the social or the economic: Bree's cohorts move spiritual capital, too, especially when they recognize and catalyze hidden resources in their own communities. And like DeAmon, Bree is quick to note that people in supposedly disinvested communities are quick to circulate economic resources for the common good—quicker than is often the case in more economically advantaged neighborhoods. She notes that her neighbors are "inherently giving, and there's this spirit of mutual aid and reciprocity and for folks that barely have anything themselves being willing to extend a helping hand to others who also don't have much."[6] That's spiritual capital in a big way: having an eye for economic resources that, for reasons of scarcity, don't seem circulatable—and yet discerning how they might be circulated anyway.

Because I met Bree late in my research process, well after my data had reached the point of saturation, I thought that conversation with her would be largely an exercise in "checking my math," making sure that my interpretation of other research data was making good sense. But I should have known that spiritual capital would surprise me again—this time in regards to the practice of storytelling pitches. Devonta Boston has complained to me that the elevator pitch is not for "relationship-building" but is rather "just-to-get-something."[7] Instead of trying to get something from outside the community through persuasive and inspirational pitch-making, Bree and her community members were practicing a kind of storytelling that I

3. "Home," Parity Homes.

4. Mattson, "On Roving & Listening in a Pandemic—DeAmon Harges."

5. Mattson, "Telling the Neighborhood Story—Bree Jones."

6. Jones, interview by author, December 15, 2020.

7. Boston, interview by author, February 14, 2020.

had not heard from others in my research interviews: she and her cohorts conduct a kind of speculative fiction as a way to make plans for neighborhood development. She told of oral storytelling events, shaped by Afro-futurism, in which her cohorts performed collective daydreaming about what they'd like to see on their properties and streets. People narrated together their aspirations for urban forests and community gardens—and sometimes more ordinary but beautifully neighborly arrangements for protecting each other's dropped-off packages. From these neighborhood storytelling events emerge committees that search out practical ways to realize these dreams. It was a mini-case study in how spiritual capital leads to social capital and then to economic capital as well.[8]

Perhaps you should shut the book right now and take the next train to Baltimore to catch one of these collective storytelling events! But then, the exact shape of such storytelling is going to vary by the organization and by the community. The narration could look conspicuously different in one of Devonta's open mic nights in Chicago Lawn or at Corey Kohn's community lunches in Boulder or at a Paint-and-Sip workshop at Charlie Branda's Art on Sedgwick in Chicago or at a Beer Thirty for the folks at Highland Solutions. But this chapter aims to provide some narrative cues for how to tell this story in your community without making the framework so tight that your community cannot speak in its own way. Following Donald Miller's construction of a heroic narrative paradigm, I'd like to sketch a paradigm that makes the Neighborhood Story tellable in your workplace and in your community in economically practicable ways.

My hope is that, after reading this chapter, you will be able to tell a fresh kind of story, shifting your organizational practices towards something besides the over-leveraged inspirational tales that tax our attentions and affections. Although that story form is quick, easy to learn, and efficient, it isn't always the best way to build a collective action.

TELLING TALES OF THE HOOD

In what follows, I unpack a new plotline of distinguishable story elements: *A neighborhood has hidden resources which catalysts quicken for community sufficiency.*

---

8. Mattson, "Telling the Neighborhood Story—Bree Jones."

A neighborhood . . .

The first challenge of any storytelling is determining the starting point for the once-upon-a-time that sets the plot in motion. What I found in talking with people like Devonta Boston or Allen Woods or Sadell Bradley was that they had generally figured out a way of comporting themselves that White investors could admire and support. Sadell called this "having to play this game to even feel that you're on the menu."[9] But I also found the lineaments of another comportment in these conversations, a narrative way of being that starts not with a hero but with a place.

Take the story of Jonathan Brooks. He can tell an inspirational story that feels straight out of the Old Testament book of Jonah. He grew up in the south Chicago neighborhood of Englewood, got out of the neighborhood to go to college and graduate school, felt called to go back to his hometown neighborhood but did not want to. He resisted the call until he could no longer bear to. But when he and his family moved in, they found beloved community. Jonathan, or "Pastah J" as his neighbors and parishioners call him, became an influential pastor, a powerful community organizer, and the author of a popular book called *Church Forsaken*. The book compares returning to one's own neighborhood with the experience of the Hebrew people going into the Babylonian Captivity. It's a disconcerting comparison. On the one hand, Englewood was his home, not his exile. But in another sense, the disinvested neighborhood had lost so much of its former glories that it did feel like exile. Pastah J felt like the prophet Jeremiah was speaking to his family with the instruction to the Hebrew people to "seek the peace of the city," making gardens, having kids, living life. Convinced that God had not forsaken Englewood, even if the church had, he joined with many others in the area to launch Kusanya Café, a social enterprise coffee shop and entrepreneurial incubator on 69th Street.

That may be the story you learn first about Pastah J. But if you sit down with him as I did over a mug of coffee and a smoothie at Kusanya Café, he'll probably start pointing out elements of the story that the inspirational narrative would bracket out. He'll point out that unlike many places in Englewood, this establishment has no bars over its windows. Kusanya seeks to maintain an open attitude to its own place. Pastah J will also tell you that if you go up to the counter and ask who owns the place, the barista will probably sing out, "You do!" The café is of the neighborhood and for the neighborhood. Jonathan will tell you to turn around and look on the wall at the back: there's a huge blackboard with all the names of the people

---

9. Bradley, interview by author, October 24, 2019.

who helped to build the place and gather its chicly hodge-podge furniture (sometimes rescuing couches from some unexpectedly resourceful dumpsters). In other words, Pastah J's story—and the narrative that this coffee shop enacts—includes more than the plot points conveyable in a website blurb. Everywhere you look, you see the story being lived out, not least in the interactions of people bent over tables, talking to each other, eating good sandwiches, making big plans.

It took me a while to figure it out, but Jonathan's testimony does not culminate in a celebration of his own perceptiveness as a social innovator, so much as in the dynamic character of the Englewood community. Nor does the church he pastors, Canaan Community Church, draw a hard line around what it does vis-à-vis what the community does. Jonathan explains it this way:

> [W]e've come to realize that what we do in the church is actually community work. Because we're a community church. So, the residents and people in the congregation are the same people. And when your congregation becomes locally based, and it's about people who walk to church from down the street and a block over and a couple blocks away, where we do work in the community, we're not doing separate work from what we're doing in church. It's the same people and it's the same work . . . And when I'm pushing to open this and all those other things, I'm not helping the community, I'm helping us. We are the community.[10]

If the first practical challenge of the Neighborhood Story is choosing where to start, Jonathan's story as it is dramatized in the coffeeshop, the church, and the community suggests this as an opening line: *Once upon a place . . .*

Although I learned to identify this element of place from the stories of people of color, a lot of my White subjects told stories that tended towards place as well. Elizabeth Biedryzcky, for example, starts the story of her work with a city, not with her own heroic vision. When she first began her work as a social entrepreneur within her Baptist denomination, she asked permission of her supervisor to spend the first months walking the streets of San Antonio, praying. This was a practice, she told me, she had learned from Shannon Hopkins, who had done the same thing in London. Elizabeth noted that walking those streets changed her prayers: "as I learn how complex our world is, my prayers become more and more simple. And my prayer for myself every day has become *God . . . help me see people the way you see them*

---

10. Brooks, interview by author, May 22, 2019.

and then help me not get in the way of that sight."[11] Sometimes, when people have told her that she should leave Texas and take her changemaker skills elsewhere, she has said: "San Antonio is my home, and this place, and being rooted in a place, is really important. I think it grounds me, and then I even got as far to others as saying I think it saves me."[12]

Charlie Branda grounds her story in place as well. Although her testimony could be interpreted as a heroic narrative, her story affirms an enfolding human interconnectedness. And this interconnectedness directs attention ultimately to an account of the hidden resources of the neighborhood along Sedgwick Avenue. She makes those resources visible by partnering with an artist to take portraits of local people. Art on Sedgwick then mounted these on large posters throughout the neighborhood saying, "You make this place beautiful." She has helped young people from nearby schools interview each other, put their stories on kites, and fly them in a local park, lifting up each other's dreams.[13] In such projects, Charlie seems to be less focused on personal overcoming and more focused on uncovering resources already present in the community.

Has Hidden Resources . . .

Here's another challenge of organizational storytelling, especially in the inspirational mode: the wicked problems that obstruct wellbeing in organizations and communities often entail structural injustice that doesn't narrate well in the hero-obstacle-mentor-plan-overcoming mode. The hero story often makes it seem that the largest problems in life are psychological. Even if there's something wrong in the system (like Neil Blumenthal uncovering the Luxotica eyeglasses monopoly), the plot moves quickly to the individual's creativity and resilience as a problem-solver. David must face down Goliath. The little under-innovator topples the corporate monopoly through entrepreneurial disruptions like the founding of Warby Parker.[14]

But the Neighborhood Story, especially as I've encountered it among people of color, must deal with non-obvious oppressiveness. There aren't Davids and Goliaths; there are places and resources. Ask Allen Woods about his work at Mortar, a Cincinnati-based accelerator focused on Black and Brown enterprise, and he's likely to launch into historical narrative, like the report of a White developer who swept into the neighborhood, bought

---

11. Biedryzcky, interview by author, February 22, 2019.
12. Biedryzcky, interview by author, February 22, 2019.
13. Branda, interview by author, June 27, 2019.
14. Blumenthal, "Warby Parker's Neil Blumenthal."

up property, sat on it for a decade until looked decrepit, then gentrified it cheaply, making a bundle in the bargain. But in Allen's telling, that developer wasn't Darth Vader. He was only an expression of a larger set of circumstances that we should call White Supremacy, circumstances which have profoundly shaped how real estate development gets done in this country.

Allen will tell you that, even as a Black man running an organization for Black-owned business development, he himself had to watch out that he didn't contribute to oppressive conditions. When he helped to launch Mortar, they spent a lot of time getting to know the area, listening to the folks who lived there. Allen says, "You got to take the time to invest in that local context and then also understand that your local context does not work everywhere." He is gesturing to the idiosyncrasies of a place, its ingenious latencies, its hidden resources.[15]

> I think everybody is trying to have this massive impact and in the thought of having massive impact they often forget the local context. For us, we still want to have massive impact, but there's baby steps to this and you can't skip the initial toddling around to try to be a marathon runner. It takes the time. You got to invest in it.[16]

One of Allen's former colleagues, Sadell Bradley, compared the way that Mortar works to a Jewish neighborhood: "the idea that here's a synagogue of people and each one of them has a different business that the whole community needs, so everyone is sustained because there's a specialization of that business and there's enough people to support the whole tribe."[17] Discovering those gifts, putting them on the map, is a large part of what the Neighborhood Story does.

This sort of narrative thus runs counter to the inspirational stories of a risktaker who has what it takes to overcome the unknown. But "what it takes" is not just grit and ingenuity, but a huge network of supporters, or as Kevin Jones might say, of wealthy aunts and uncles. This "invisible capital," to use Chris Rabb's useful term, rarely gets talked about. As Allen explains,

> When White people fail in tech, it's fail fast, and go try again. You'll find more investors to invest in your next idea. But we don't get multiple opportunities to fail. You get that one good time. And then the thing is, *you* get that one time to fail, but your one time to fail is often the only time to fail for the entire

15. Woods, interview by author, June 11, 2020.
16. Woods, interview by author, June 11, 2020.
17. Bradley, interview by author, October 24, 2019.

group. So, it's not, "Hey, you failed once, but we believe in you, so we'll fund you again." It's, "I heard about somebody who tried to do this once who looked like you, and they failed. So, I don't want to take the risk."[18]

Belonging to place and community is always complicated, as the Mortar stories make clear: on the one hand, your neighbors provide a needed support network; on the other hand, you carry the burden of your neighbors' wellbeing. If you fail, it reflects on them.

This combination of precarity and belonging results in a fresh kind of storytelling, one in which risk is not individually celebrated but communally distributed. The goal isn't just to persuade (or bluff) a donor or investor into underwriting a brilliantly finessed and daringly executed gambler, a card-sharp James-Bond figure out of *Casino Royale*. Instead, the Neighborhood Story seeks to make apparent and shareable the hidden resources that will enable a community, as Wendell Berry might say, to recognize itself as members of each other. As Allen explains,

> I think that contextually, specifically in the Black church, there will be people who, no matter what level of poverty you come from, they will measure by faith and not by bank account . . . So, like feeding the people who are around you. Giving even of your last to make sure that community-wise, everybody's good.[19]

Mapping the hidden resources that are so subtly there is a way to circulate spiritual capital, a feel for the practical economic possibilities that come from mutuality and membership.

Because the Neighborhood Story is just as persuasively *experienced* as it is told, sometimes the best way to get people to tell the story is to get them to live it. When Shannon Hopkins looks at a wicked social problem like sex trafficking, she could tell an inspirational story about heroically rescuing women from what is essentially slavery. But instead of telling a pathos-drenched story, she designed a game that helped organizational communities recognize the barely visible resources that might contribute to positive change.[20] Or to cite another example, when DeAmon Harges talks about social banking, he can hardly keep from talking about meals. He sees the practice of eating together not just as a metaphor that describes vibrant community but also as practice that constitutes community. What makes a difference in the world, suggests Tobias Jones, is "not tidal wave thinking"

18. Woods, interview by author, June 11, 2020.

19. Woods, interview by author, June 11, 2020.

20. "Shannon Hopkins: The gamification of innovation," *Faith & Leadership*.

so much as dwelling with folks "preferably under the same roof with their knees under the same table."[21] Such practice can be scandalizing, especially when it is done, as DeAmon recommends, with the very perpetrators of harm. But even when the practice is small-scaled and scandalous, it can be surprisingly efficacious as a means of counter-cultural storytelling. "Having a meal and a party with your enemies is a sign of protest," he suggests, insisting that such meals are more vital than "going to the statehouse."[22]

Which Catalysts Quicken . . .

A practical challenge in organizational storytelling is that marketing and fundraising and development stories all contend with a massively crowded mediascape. Jonathan Crary has noted that "there will always be something online more informative, surprising, funny, diverting, impressive than anything in one's immediate actual circumstances."[23] As a result, the great threat to any inspirational story is the intrusion of a hundred more diverting messages ready to hand. But the Neighborhood Story, in a way, depends upon interruptions. Because it decenters the teller, it relies upon other actants, other contributors, other voices to give it sense and power.

While we were sitting at a Kusanya table talking about change in Englewood, Jonathan looked up and saw a young businesswoman at the counter, who came over and gave him a joyous hug. As it turned out, hers was the first nonprofit Kusanya was not only incubating but hosting in their space upstairs: Growing Home, the only USDA-certified urban farm in Chicago. Way leads on to way, as Robert Frost would say—and those ways led me to interview, for the podcast *Spiritual Capital*, the executive director of that organization, Janelle St. John. In a vital sense, I could not understand Jonathan's Kusanya story without hearing from the folks at Growing Home. But Janelle in turn emphasized that she could not understand her own organizational story unless it was interrupted by narratives from the neighborhood. Nonprofits have to respond to their neighborhood, she insisted, even if doing that looks like mission creep. That's okay, she says, let the place shape your mission. People like Pastah J and Janelle are catalysts, because their aim is not to superimpose their own competencies on a neighborhood, but rather to release the neighborhood's capacities toward the common good.[24]

---

21. Jones, interview by author, April 24, 2019.
22. Harges, interview by author, April 13, 2020.
23. Crary, 24/7, 60.
24. Mattson, "Kohlrabi Capital—Janelle St. John."

Although the term *catalyst* is widely recognized in community initiatives, I credit Dave Odom for alerting me to the usefulness of this term.[25] His description of this peculiar vocation makes me think of catalysts as human embodiments of spiritual capital. They are not only able to animate capital; they are themselves among the assets of a community—although they are often awaiting activation, so to speak, by others who recognize their unconventional or hidden giftedness. But it's hard to talk about this community role; it's hard to narrate it—apart, that is, from something like the Neighborhood Story. In his work at Duke's *Faith & Leadership,* Dave has conceptualized the *catalyst* in an often hard-to-define role within organizational life. Alongside the entrepreneurial "adventurers" and the establishmentarian "investors," there are also those figures who help to animate and mediate other people's gifts. These people

> are often behind the scenes when something good is happening. They have an eye for talented people and can envision how people with a diversity of gifts can accomplish significant work together. Catalysts often have considerable intellectual or organizational savvy that they use for the benefit of others . . . Catalysts' default is to encourage, connect and release. They spark activity and then typically step away. After their projects become successful and begin to scale, it is often difficult to recognize that they have been there.[26]

Dave told me when I interviewed him that there were catalysts in the 1970s and 1980s who worked in church settings, often invisibly or incomprehensibly. "They were wonderful. Their jobs were nearly impossible to understand, and so some people thought of it as political. And sometimes it had that dimension to it. They were trying to change social conditions, so they were considered whatever, liberal or something. But they did their work so that others flourished."[27] The waning influence of the organized church has resulted, however, in denomination cutbacks, which made free-agents of these catalysts. Today, Dave works with others at Duke on Reflective Leadership grants to catalyze the catalysts, to release the release agents, enabling them to do their inconspicuous but vital work.

At the same conference where I interviewed Dave, I met a catalytic peer of his, DeAmon Harges. He told me pretty quickly that he doesn't so much like to be asked "What do you do?" He'd prefer if somebody said, "Tell me your story." And it's a question he's quick to ask other as well. In fact,

25. Odom, interview by author, October 23, 2019. See also Odom, "How to Nurture."
26. Odom, "How to Nurture."
27. Odom, interview by author, October 23, 2019.

when he slides his business card across the table, it features an unusual title: "Roving Listener." How does he perform this vocation? He goes around to his neighbors, asking simple, human questions like, "When was the last time you gave something away without expecting anything in return?" Or he'll ask, "Tell me the story of how you were born." He's listening for answers that give him a sense of the neighborhood, or as he likes to put it, the ecology. Often people don't know what to do with his questions: "I would always go personal first. 'Who shaped your convictions?' . . . And then, professionals will go, 'Well, I do this, and I do that.' I say, 'No, no, no, tell me about your mother.' That usually informs me."[28] What he's listening for in all this is the presence of gifts in the community. He celebrates "[t]he idea that you need witnesses and help promote other witnesses, because the truth of the matter is, if there's any need it's all of us . . . to be needed, right?"[29]

DeAmon is a shrewd social analyst. His work in philanthropy helps him to read people quickly and to understand the ins and outs of fiscal structures. But he's not looking for what's going wrong; he's looking for what's going right but is overlooked. To explain how this works, let me cite his own example: "If you had ten heart attacks, it's nothing I can do with that, oh sister, oh brother. Hey, but you know what? You throw the best parties I know. I'm gonna bring some friends over. You know what I mean?"[30] What energizes him is the sense that giving is always, already going on, often in hidden ways. He talks about the affection and generosity that circulates in his neighborhood.

> That's what God's economy looks like. Fiscal capital develops out of there. I think that's it. How many times have we counted the philanthropy in a low-income neighborhood? . . . Not often enough.[31]

What moves him is people who give and keep giving for decades at a time even without hope of return. He likes to retell the story of the widow of Zarephath whom Elijah instructed to go get pots from her neighbors. She collected a few, but Elijah's miracle filled all the pots with the oil the woman needed to live. The story implies that if she had drawn even more trustfully on the resourcefulness of her neighbors, borrowing more of their pots, she would have found an answering generosity in God's provision.

---

28. Harges, interview by author, April 13, 2020.
29. Harges, interview by author, April 13, 2020.
30. Harges, interview by author, April 13, 2020.
31. Mattson, "On Roving & Listening in a Pandemic—DeAmon Harges."

What makes DeAmon a catalyst, besides his feel for philanthropic circulations in overlooked places, is his knack for connecting people. He's a steroidal networker. *You really ought to talk to this person. Let me tell you about my friend Mike. Here's somebody else you should meet.* His aim is to put gifts into circulation, to pull goods into relationship, to be constantly transferring spiritual capital from hand to hand.

I think another element of the catalyst that strikes me is her or his keen sense of productive inappropriateness in one's vocation. To be a catalyst is not to hold a recognizable expertise. A lot of my interviewees, in fact, were doing things they weren't trained to do or didn't feel up for. Jonathan felt this way when he took over the church in Englewood, for example. Corey Kohn had always understood herself as a creative, a producer, a film-editor, not a businessperson. Emily Lonigro and Demetrio Maguigad had both seen themselves as activists—and now found themselves running a company. But as a catalyst, DeAmon sees his incapacities as leverage. Often, he fulfils the role of a community journalist, capturing, recording people's stories. But he explains, "I'm terribly at notetaking. I don't physically write; I do this or have somebody transcribe." But even here, in trying to compensate for a felt incapacity, he sees opportunity. By bringing along a transcriber, he subtly recruits another witness: "Inadvertently, they get to see into the practice."[32]

For Community Sufficiency . . .

Telling good stories takes good money. When some students of mine consulted with a pro-social bakery in Chicago, they rather innocently recommended upgrades to her digital presence. But making those changes, as she helped my students to understand, takes time and money. And when you're trying to make a couple dozen pies for a banquet the next day, while training your workers to be the consummate professionals of the day after that, well, there isn't always enough world and time to tell your inspirational stories better on Instagram. Besides, creating more and more marketing messages can be a way of participating in what Crary has called 24/7, which, he says, "is inseparable from environmental catastrophe in its declaration of permanent expenditure, of endless wastefulness for its sustenance, in its terminal disruption of the cycles and seasons on which ecological integrity depends."[33]

There is, however, a surprising thriftiness to the Neighborhood Story, and not just because its practitioners are capable of fiduciary self-restraint.

32. Mattson, "On Roving & Listening in a Pandemic—DeAmon Harges."
33. Crary, 24/7, 10.

I did hear, of course, organizational stories of conventional thrift—stories like Jonathan's hilarious tale of dumpster-diving for the surprisingly chic furniture now ensconced in Kusanya Café.[34] But the sufficiency that the Neighborhood Story has us explore is not simply an organization's report on its own innovative use of resources. The sufficiency of the Neighborhood Story is something enacted, not reported.

For Thomas Princen, sufficiency is the commonsense principle that when you've had enough, you stop. He notes that it makes no sense at all to burn through resources out of a weirdly shortsighted devotion to maximal efficiency, which in turn leads to power abuse and massive possibilities for deception.[35] And that brings us to inspirational storytelling, which is, in a certain sense, highly efficient and yet prone to a maximalist logic. Its efficiency rests in its address to the listener's psychology cleanly, quickly, sparely. Adam Neumann, formerly of WeWork, was a highly efficient inspirational storyteller, in that sense of the term: he managed to achieve prodigious wealth through a narrative form that, at first hearing, sounds like Neighborhood Storytelling. Neumann spoke often of the importance of collaboration and cooperation, emphasized the role of place in everyday work, and centered his rhetoric on the vitality of community. His storytelling worked efficiently, garnering nearly $10 billion from SoftBank's Masayoshi Son. Unfortunately, WeWork proved to be a massively over-leveraged firm, hemorrhaging so much cash that Neumann was forced to step down as CEO. Masayoshi Son later said, "My investment judgment was poor in many ways. I am reflecting deeply on that." He noted, "I overestimated Neumann's good side . . . I have learned a harsh lesson."[36] Princen would certainly agree. The story is just the sort of wasteful expression of the logic of efficiency he deplores. Neumann's gauzy, spiritually inflected communitarianism was profoundly *insufficient*. Still, the problem with Princen is that he distinguishes too sharply between stories lived and stories told, whereas

34. Brooks, interview by author, May 22, 2019.

35. Our devotion to this taken-for-granted notion is hardly surprising, of course, given how pervasively efficiency has come to shape institutional and even personal life today. During the twentieth century, Princen notes, everything from household management to manufacturing to politics gradually gave nearly total allegiance to efficiency. Of course, a certain kind of efficiency can be a good thing, especially when it is a tool to achieve a good end. But when efficiency becomes not just an instrument but a whole way of living, it leverages a potentially swollen power to do harm: "And those who can manipulate the techniques, those who claim the efficiencies, gain the advantage. Far from removing politics from government, let alone from any other realm—the company, the church, the forest, the river—efficiency creates its own politics." Princen, *The Logic of Sufficiency*, 72.

36. Jolly, "SoftBank boss takes blame."

the Neighborhood Story conjoins the two.[37] The organization itself becomes the story lived and the story told.

I think I detected this organization-as-story when practitioners went out of their way to avoid hype. Jon Berbaum is a successful social business-person, but he leaves no room for uncanny optimism in his ways of talking about his company's engagement with the predicaments of our time. "I in no way see business and capitalistic business as the savior of the problems that we've created for ourselves." He asks, "Am I participating in this wealthy self-delusion of 'Oh no, this is great we can keep doing the stuff we're doing and just do good instead'?" He describes the "hand waving" that goes on in social entrepreneurship as a worrisomely self-delusional phenomenon.[38] Jon still engages social business as a force for good, but when he looks at the latent capacities of his community, he sees mostly the potential to make a good product and to offer care for human wellbeing. As the company's website notes in its genuine and matter-of-fact tone: "We believe that what we create should make it a little bit better to be alive: for us, our clients, and their customers."[39]

Corey Kohn's stories, too, resist the hype of inspirationalism and embrace the down-to-earth-ness of good neighboring and good work. When her company, DOJO4, made its first aspirational turn towards social enterprise, the company took a high-minded route: they committed to working exclusively with pro-social enterprises—a riskily heroic course of action. But that story shifted to a less heroic register eventually. Corey and her colleagues figured out that other companies' pro-social missions aren't always effective, aren't always worth supporting. Besides, adds Corey, should a social enterprise let its moral purity keep it from interacting with profit-driven corporations? On top of doing good work and making worthwhile digital products, Corey's company seeks another unhyped good: making a good place to work. Doing that, allows them to move into healthy and hospitable relationship with their adjacent community, especially when they host luncheons: "Sometimes there's four of us and other times like today, we had twenty people . . . We order a big lunch and then we offer that to

---

37. I am appropriating these terms from the communication theorists Pearce and Cronen, whose Coordinated Management of Meaning theory distinguished, for therapeutic purposes, the ways that people live and the ways that they talk later about that living. See Griffin, et al., *A First Look at Communication*. The move I am making in this paragraph I learned from Rickert who both critiqued Princen and described a rhetoric that was also a way of dwelling. See Rickert, *Ambient Rhetoric*.

38. Berbaum, interview by author, May 2, 2019.

39. "Highland," Highland Solutions.

our community. There's dogs and kids and it's so sweet. It feels plentiful."[40] Again and again, my early interpretation of heroically inspirational organizational narratives had to shift towards what Mark Sampson of Rooted Good describes as "less about solving a problem and more about creating an opportunity for . . . *neighboring*."[41]

Sometimes living out the Neighborhood Story means paying attention to the tedious taken-for-granteds of organizational life. Only by watching those infrastructural details closely could the non-human actants in a workplace come into clear relief.[42] At Lime Red Studio, Emily Lonigro keeps a sharp eye out for what documents are doing in her company. She describes herself as "a big believer in the operational documents of a business and how they are designed to be inequitable." For example, she hates what she sees as the unethical impersonality of Requests for Proposals. She also eliminated non-competes years ago, because of their unfairness. "How can you say, 'You can't work for anyone in a related field in our city for a year—it's just ridiculous to think that in this world." When it comes to hiring processes, she lobbied against the requirement to disclose salary history, which disadvantage women and people of color. "It's not fair to perpetuate that."[43] Because the Neighborhood story involves places and resources as much as people, attention to organizational algorithms is unavoidable.

Emily told me a story about how she had been ready to close a deal with a woman business owner, who was contracting to do a job for Lime Red. But Emily said the woman was clearly under-charging, adhering tacitly to the mainstream economic norms in which women regularly undervalue the worth of their own services. Emily could have, in that moment, justifiably said that she could not afford to expend the attention, that she had no time to tell others how to manage their accounts. The same economy that was pressuring the contractor to under-charge was also pressuring Emily to expend her the scarce capital of her awareness—on simply keeping up with the overwhelming demands of a truly frightening email inbox. But as a woman business owner, mindful that a male-dominated field often disadvantages women, she decided to stare at the paperwork for a while and figure out a more equitable contractual arrangement. She told the contractor that she would pay nearly three times what she'd been asked to and that

40. Kohn, interview by author, May 10, 2019.

41. Sampson, interview by author, October 24, 2019.

42. The term *actant* is often associated with Latour, *Reassembling the Social,* 54–55.

43. Mattson, "The Spirit in the Details—Emily Lonigro."

if more were needed, she'd pay that, too. Living the Neighborhood Story entails enacting the sufficiency of acting justly.[44]

THE GENIUS OF THE PLACE

I have been implying that the Neighborhood Story is a good option for your organization, something to consider if you grow weary of the pabulum of the inspirational narrative. But given large-scale institutional breakdowns across mainstream society, the sort of breakdowns that make social entrepreneurships like Bree Jones's Parity Homes indispensable—well, your organization, whatever it is, will almost certainly need to learn how to tell the Neighborhood Story in the near future.

Let's say you help run a for-profit corporation. If your corporate social responsibility initiatives are to be anything but perfunctory, you're going to have to be grounded in *place*. Let's say you run a religious organization or lead a church. Your denomination or your local church almost certainly enjoys much less influence than the mainstream church did seventy years back in American life. And that means that you're looking at the *hidden resourcefulness* of your church building anew, asking how spaces used once or twice a week for congregations might also serve incubators and enterprises.[45] Let's say that you are a faculty member in higher education. You notice that your college's marketing materials tout job-ready degrees, a promise that can be hard to deliver through the conventional routes of peer-reviewed research. But the Neighborhood Story encourages faculty members to see themselves not as the mentors for their students' heroic journeys, but rather as *the catalysts* who help these students attach to networks of practical engagement and world-betterment. The massive social and ecological problems closing in on business-as-usual approaches to the world mean that organizations of all kinds are needing to set aside uncannily optimistic preoccupations with efficiency and to embrace *sufficiency* instead.

The social entrepreneurs I spoke with in this chapter have figured out Bree Jones's insight, that organizational leadership entails more than shrewd business strategies on the one hand or therapeutic people care on the other. Neither of these is sufficient for wellbeing in your organization and your organization's community. Instead, when these leaders seek to run their organization well and engage their communities well, they build ingenious memberships, some of whom are corporate figures, some of whom work for religious organizations, some of whom are faculty and student researchers,

44. Mattson, "The Spirit in the Details—Emily Lonigro."
45. Eldson, *We Aren't Broke.*

some of whom are entrepreneurs. The genius at play in these networks of changemaking is not the individual's capacity to innovate or imagine, but instead the *genius* that David Whyte recovers in the ancient Latin sense: *genius loci*, or "spirit of the place." This chapter has sought to narrate the spirit of the neighborhood, where, in Whyte's terms, we find "a unique signature, inherited from our ancestors, our landscape, our language, and beneath it, a half-hidden geology of existence: memories, hurts, triumphs, and stories in our lineage that have not yet been fully told."[46]

46. Whyte, *Consolations*, 78.

6

Expanding the Range of Our Affections

LET ME START WITH two stories about organizations and their neighborhoods.

One day Robert White and I stepped out of Cara's office and into—if memory serves—a bitter Chicago day on Desplaines Avenue. We had just finished a long conversation, and to keep things going just a few minutes longer, he'd offered to walk me down to my car. He and I have interviewed numerous times, and there never seems to be enough time for the conversations. So I was glad for his company. As we hurried across an intersection, we encountered a man asking for spare cash. I think because I had just come out of a nonprofit organization dedicated to fighting poverty—and, yes, perhaps because I was in the company of an interviewee—I reached for my wallet. But Robert did not. Instead, he asked the man a few questions and then encouraged him to connect with Cara's program. He turned and pointed to the building.

I remember feeling sheepish about what my small change had offered the man in comparison with what Robert had afforded by way of practical advice and meaningful organizational assistance. But the fact that the man needed to be told about Cara, an establishment with a long and storied history, just a few buildings away, also caught my attention. Maybe the man was only thinking about cash. But the fact that he *appeared* at any rate not to know about Cara reminded me of challenges faced by organizations seeking to live out the Neighborhood Story described in the last chapter.

Bryan Ungard proved to be the sort of business leader willing to play hooky from a conference session one sunny forenoon in April. We sat on a low wall outside the conference center in the Scotts Valley sunlight and within earshot of wind chimes. It was a time and place inviting low-voiced conversation—in Bryan's case not about social enterprise, but about his for-profit movie theatre. He tries to run his company in a conscious way in keeping with what he sees as the universe's levels of engagement: the vital level, where we do what we have to do to survive; the automatic level, where habits reign; the sensitive level, where a basic mindfulness sets in; and the conscious level, where we live from our source and towards our true purpose. For the longest time, he had thought his company's mission might be to help his employees move from merely vital to fully conscious engagements.

When he interviewed teenagers for employment, he played the Socratic gadfly, teasing them out with indirect questions. "Tell me about the times that you're energized. Tell me about times when you feel like you're more yourself. Tell me about times when you don't feel more yourself, when you feel stuck and heavy and blocked."[1] Once the teenager got over the surprise at being asked questions at this level of discernment, she or he might start providing what Bryan called "clues," directional guidance that would help to make a cineplex a meaningful place of work.[2] "If I'm being less filtered, I'll say, what's the role that you're being called to play? What is your calling? What is your vocation, capital V?"[3]

But then, a half dozen years ago or so, he came into a fuller sense of mission. As he explained simply, he realized that "oh crap, we touch a lot of people in the world."[4] This new awareness for an unexpectedly personal relationality led him to a new sort of wisdom question: "Do we have some accountability or opportunity to create places for those people to flourish as well?"[5]

I start with these two examples, one a nonprofit and the other a for-profit company, to identify an aspiration and an accountability felt by more and more organizations to their place, to their adjacent communities. They aspire for what Chris Rabb calls "commonwealth entrepreneurship," in that they ask not just about their own profitability and sustainability but "whether the enterprise improves the broad sustainability of the community in which it operates—including the internal community of stakeholders

1. Ungard, interview by author, April 12, 2019.
2. Ungard, interview by author, April 12, 2019.
3. Ungard, interview by author, April 12, 2019.
4. Ungard, interview by author, April 12, 2019.
5. Ungard, interview by author, April 12, 2019.

without which the enterprise could not survive."[6] They try not just to tell, but also to live out what the last chapter called the Neighborhood Story.

But this sort of engagement is enormously challenging. Ask Jonathan Brooks in Englewood, Allen Woods in Cincinnati, Charlie Branda on Sedgwick Avenue, Devonta Boston in Chicago Lawn, and Bree Jones in West Baltimore, and they can tick off the challenges for organizations and their leaders in neighborhood engagement:

- Organizations work hard to differentiate their projects and achievements from that of other organizations. In contrast with these tightly defined boundaries, neighborhoods are often vaguely defined.[7]

- Organizations often have a light step and can change course quickly; neighborhoods rarely can. Organizational changefulness has disconcerted me more than once even in the course of this research: companies downsize or expand; business models alter; brand expressions change; people move up, down, or out of their company hierarchies. But in neighborhoods, bringing meaningful change can take a long time.[8]

- Organizations keep accountable to diverse standards and approaches within their own accounting, management, HR, and marketing. But neighborhood engagements require an even more diverse accountability with locals who know better than you what needs to be done in a neighborhood.[9]

Of course, virtual neighborhood interactions are no less complicated. Not all of my interview subjects enjoy direct involvement in their place. They might be working in a cubicle in an incubator hub on a largely industrialized boulevard, keeping shop twenty-five stories up in the Chicago

6. Rabb, *Invisible Capital*, 143.

7. Often in the city contexts where social entrepreneurs do their work, "boundaries between neighborhoods are almost always inexorably porous and are often somewhat blurred." Meagher, "A Neighbourhood Vitality Index," 5. I am reliant in these three bullet points upon Meagher, whose scholarship has helped me to un-skein the challenges woven subtly through my interview data with place-based enterprises.

8. "Practitioners often cite 3–5 year time frames . . . Few practitioners and even fewer funders are willing to wait that long to determine if they are on the right track." Meagher, "A Neighbourhood Vitality Index," 7.

9. I remember riding on the back of a moped from house to house in Pignon, Haiti, watching as Haitian field researchers tried to learn local priorities. But even for indigenous researchers, the data could be challenging to interpret. None of the community members we talked to admitted going to the witchdoctor when they felt sick. All claimed to go to the health clinic. But given the popularity of Vudu in Haiti, this data was, at the very least, ambiguous.

Board of Trade building, or negotiating consultancies from Hawaii for folks in Kansas. My own college is constantly talking about the importance of place but struggles to define the exact site for place-based engagement: should our institutional engagements be in our own wealthy suburb or in less prosperous suburbs ten minutes away or in the neighborhoods of Chicago half an hour to the north of us? As I discussed in the chapter on dialogue, digital neighboring isn't less personal or invested, simply because it's not face-to-face. In fact, as Peters has argued, what we think of as authentic, interpersonal dialogue can reveal profound gaps between people who had thought themselves intimates.[10] Conversations with organizational leaders like Corey Kohn in Boulder, Jon Berbaum in Chicago, and Maiken Piil in Copenhagen have impressed me that organizational leaders have to be creative in their definition of their organization's neighborhoods—which makes such engagements, again, notably complicated:

- Organizations need to be able to prioritize their projects. But if they are building relationships with digital communities, it can be hard to know why *this* community as opposed to *that* one. Whose needs have priority?[11]

- Organizations that specialize in digital work may find that their usual products and services are financially out of reach for communities in need.[12]

- Organizations navigating digital environments must deal with the deleterious effects of the mainstream attention economy, especially in the ways that the people they are seeking to help are already overwhelmed by digital messaging.

Both those who engage their neighborhoods physically and those who do so virtually need spiritual capital, especially if they are going to avoid

10. "We all tend to resist acknowledging the fundamental gap at the heart of all discourse, even though negotiating the gap is a daily accomplishment most adult language-users are quite expert at," writes Peters, whose scholarship has profoundly shaped this book's analysis and reflections. "The physical presence of another is no guarantee that 'communication' will happen." See Peters, "The Gaps," 131.

11. While working on the latter parts of this book, I became invested in a socially entrepreneurial network that connected my college with a diffuse network of catalysts, including Jon Berbaum, all for the purpose of cultivating homeowner resilience in South Chicago. But a significant part of our work has been defining where a good point of intervention might be.

12. I am grateful for the chance to think about digital communicational challenges with Thompson, *The Virtual Body of Christ* and to my colleague Bethany Keeley-Jonker's excellent review of the book: Keeley-Jonker, "The Virtual Body of Christ," 305–7.

paternalistic community interventions. They need, in other words, to recognize that there are already economic resources and social networks at play in their communities. Spiritual capital helps them to recognize these often-subtle forms of capital and, as this chapter will relate, to catalyze them.

IMPACT CHAINS

Many, if not most, community initiatives start by asking what resources are needed in a community and how they might bring them there. This process often gets depicted with the metaphor of an impact value chain, as organizers sketch out a plan for linking inputs and outputs to outcomes and impact. The metaphor of the impact value chain derives from the widely appropriated Information Systems Model, developed by Shannon Weaver in the 1950s to explain how (among other things) communication happens: the Sender encodes Information, transmits it along a Channel to a Receiver, and achieves some measurable Effect.

The impact value chain, however, often fails to fully account for the causal sequencing of community betterment. "This is partially because the mechanisms of change are not obvious," notes Sean Meagher, "and it is hard to legitimately claim that events that follow interventions are caused by those interventions without a clear causal chain of events."[13] Just as sending and receiving information does not necessarily explain the construction of shared *meaning*, so inputs and outputs do not map out a sequence leading to the qualitative event of community *transformation*. Logicians call it a pleonastic fallacy when incremental steps purportedly lead to some wholly new emergence. (The rest of us just call this magical thinking.)

To get around these sometimes-dubious causal linkages, some theories of change multiply community inputs, expanding the democratic processes of stakeholder conversations, working painstakingly towards consensus about likely causes and likely effects. In such well-intentioned deliberations, the changemakers seek to build agreement that if *this* short-term input is conducted and *that* short-term outcome happens, then *this* long-term outcome will also eventually happen—*right, everybody?*[14] Theories of change tend to adhere to an admirably democratic process, even if they

---

13. Meagher, "A Neighborhood Vitality Index," 8.

14. Construing community-betterment projects traces to work on theories of change in Weiss, "Nothing as Practical as Good Theory." My own engagement with this approach draws on Connell and Kubisch, "Applying a Theory."

underestimate how wealth and privilege make it easier for some people to participate in democratic conversations than for others.[15]

STICKY AFFECTIONS

Put differently, these highly rational processes can underestimate the role of collective feelings in the deliberative conversation. I don't just mean personal feelings (*I feel tired or afraid or disgusted*); nor do I mean simply counting up all the feelings in the room (*She feels happy, he feels fearful, they feel excited*). Instead, following Condit, I refer to collective feelings, a third emotional social structure, which she synopsizes as the "motivating affects focused around collective action."[16] Such collective feeling when attached to an organizational-neighborhood project can be longer-lasting than personal emotions. One person's moods pass quickly; but the feelings that accompany a community initiative can be and "must be sustainable across periods of quiescence, and yet remain activatable as the timetables for executing collective actions demand."[17] Collective feelings, as Sara Ahmed would say, are highly adhesive.[18]

I remember joining a Black Lives Matter rally in the summer of 2020 and then, after the rally, walking back through a quiet, largely White neighborhood for a mile and a half to my car. Moms and dads and strollers passed, smiling and side-eyeing my BLM sign. Kids swarmed by on their bikes. I felt even more conspicuous on that walk than I had during the protest in the middle of Cal-Sag Avenue, shouting out Breonna Taylor's name. Walking through that neighborhood, I sensed that my BLM sign was out of place; but the collective indignation of the rally against racial inequity had stuck the sign to me nonetheless. When I got home, I still couldn't let it go, so I stuck it in our front yard.

Sara Ahmed suggests that "stickiness" is precisely how collective feelings work. Feelings are adhesives. They attach economic and social goods

15. Some critics of such deliberative fora, notes Condit, actually "become part of the forces of oppression because groups that are historically or economically advantaged are better able to participate and succeed in the process of democratic deliberation." Condit, *Angry Public Rhetorics,* 232.

16. "Collective emotion in this sense is more than simply the sum of the emotional predispositions of individuals for three reasons: (1) it requires collective identities; (2) it necessitates the enunciation of motivating affects focused around collective action; (3) the circulatory systems that are the media and other social structures unevenly amplify the feelings of different individuals or groups." Condit, *Angry Public Rhetorics,* 65.

17. Condit, *Angry Public Rhetorics,* 66.

18. Ahmed, *The Cultural Politics of Emotion,* 89–92.

to each other and to people and move the goods around in a society.[19] A corporation uses a social media video, for example, to attach a brand logo to something (a truck, a pair of running shoes, a baby monitor). As people watch the video, collective desire for that thing puts it into circulation. The action of emotion sticks to more than physical capital. I remember after the 2010 earthquake in Haiti, hearing that social entrepreneurial leaders in Les Cayes needed more than physical resources. The Haitian leaders were also yearning for social resources. When North American doctors and pastors showed up—simply arriving on the border of the Dominican Republic ready to ride a bus to Les Cayes—that was itself a way to make social capital visible. It was as if the Haitian leaders simply wanted to say, "We have people." And having people required collective feelings of compassion to attach social networks in the U.S. and in Haiti with a strong bond.

These feelings, however, do not simply create adhesion; they also involve movement. Sometimes, these collective affections and their stickiness can move a lot of capital: when a U.S. President delivers a speech that provokes collective wrath against an adversary, that emotion moves through the country rapidly—and moves enormous amounts of military resources as well. When twenty-four-hour coverage of a tsunami activates collective compassion, all kinds of physical resources move too: building supplies, crates of food, and blood banks. Ahmed notes that "stickiness involves a form of relationality, or a 'withness', in which the elements that are 'with' get bound together. One can stick by a friend. One can get stuck in traffic. Some forms of stickiness are about holding things together. Some are about blockages or stopping things moving."[20] Collective feelings of disgust can block the movement of resources. Collective feelings of empathy or hatred can attach and move resources.

One sticky emotion I have repeatedly put in question throughout this book is the spirituality-infused hopefulness that I have called uncanny optimism. Such optimism can be hugely adhesive, and changemakers are understandably glad to feel it. But as the experience of Bree Jones and others have made clear, the fact that one person feels an energizing sanguinity about the future is, of course, no assurance that it would be productive for everyone in a given community to feel exactly that optimism.[21] Optimism as a collective mover of social and economic capital has its shortcomings. It can be naïve about cause and effect, as when changemakers assume too

19. Ahmed, *The Cultural Politics of Emotion*, 89–92.

20. Ahmed, *The Cultural Politics of Emotion*, 91.

21. As Condit points out, having a feeling does not oblige sharing that feeling with others: "To insist on linking one's felt experience with one's public interactions might be called the self-expression fallacy." Condit, *Angry Public Rhetorics*, 219

quickly that *this* will directly lead to *that.* Optimism can posit who's in and who's out in a community: *If you feel cheerful about this plan, you're in. If not, well, we're not going to tell you to find another community, but—*. Optimism can also be impatient with other feelings, tending not to interact with feelings of sadness or ordinary happiness in the midst of everyday conditions. Its future-orientation can disable lament, confession, rejoicing, repentance, or reparation, attributing to these actions a politics of despair or sloth or cynicism. *You're just sad, because you're hopeless. You're happy because you're lazy. You despair because you're cynical.*

Although optimism's uncanny efficiency *seems* like a good way to connect a plan for community engagement with social and economic capital, its affiliations can be too narrow, and its inclinations too heedless of history, too neglectful of the fact that, "communities have a rich array of emotions—disgust, compassion, joy, fear, or sadness—by which to regulate their interactions."[22] These various emotions are ready to hand, like glue sticks in a desk drawer. But although we tend to reach for the optimism glue stick first when we're engaging a neighborhood, there are other viable adhesives with fewer of the side effects of uncanny optimism.

SPIRITUAL CAPITAL AGAIN

This final chapter asks a spiritual capital question. How do we catalyze resources, whether economic or social, for the sake of the communities where our organizations do their work? Because this question assumes that resources are often treasures hidden in a field, the query differs from those asked in impact value chain thinking. Value-chain thinking tends to treat resources as transparently accountable: either the economic and social capital is there, or it's not. Spiritual capital, though, has us asking how resources get noticed in the first place. Goods can be very present in a community without being noticed, sometimes because they have been deliberately hidden, as in the case of real estate developers who want to obscure the possibilities in a set of buildings for eventual gentrification. But resources can be simply latent, because no one has activated them within the community and for the community's good. In past chapters, I have focused on spiritual capital as a way of seeing overlooked goods in a workplace or in a community; in this chapter, I focus on spiritual capital's capability to activate and circulate those overlooked goods. If the last chapter zeroed in on how spiritual capital is a manner of seeing, a way of paying attention, often via the Neighborhood

22. Condit, *Angry Public Rhetorics,* 223.

Story, this chapter attends to the second part of the concept: how spiritual capital can move those resources within a neighborhood.

Here's what the rest of this chapter wishes to argue: organizations seeking the wellbeing of their communities need a variety of collective feelings to package and circulate social and economic capital. Optimism is a go-to activator for community betterment projects for understandable reasons. But spiritual capital can also arrive with other sorts of affect: joy, delight, love, belonging, and surprise. These diverse feelings, as they move, create similarly diverse routes for capital to move around. As playful delight, abiding love, or surprising generosity create pathways, these feelings move socio-economic capital throughout a community. A quick example of this: economically disadvantaged communities are often shown to practice more generosity than their wealthier counterparts. The people in these communities know how to see unlooked-for goods. But they also allow themselves the usual varied affections of neighborly interactions in everyday life. That's what neighboring does: rejoicing with those who rejoice, weeping with those who weep, laughing with those who laugh, delighting with those who delight, getting mad with those who get mad, and so on. And as those feelings circulate, so do goods.

I began this project with earnest interview questions about spiritual practices related to awareness, wisdom, generosity, and so on. I conclude the project by showing that the feelings accompanying these practices can and do become collective and how their collectivity creates routes for all kinds of capital to circulate. The social entrepreneurs I interviewed ran their organizations as what you might call emotional path-makers, and their pathways were remarkably varied. I'll discuss just four of the kinds of affective walkways that they have helped to create in their communities, nicknaming these structures Gamification, Encounter, Church, and Gift.[23]

GAMIFICATION

I have twice participated in the game called Mission Possible, once as a player, once as a judge. On both occasions, the players took their place at various tables scattered around a large room—the first being a theatre, the second a gymnasium. Each team had to select a type of wicked problem, a social or ecological predicament not traceable to one perpetrator nor resolvable in quick and linear fashion. Once the problem area is selected, the team narrows the crisis to a specific predicament. Each team of problem-solvers

---

23. I am indebted to Jenkins's discussions of modes, affect, and circulation for this discussion of ways of interfacing.

is given a set of quirky resources to use in addressing this problem. For example, they might be given a big-top tent and one hundred inflatable rafts and $250. Perhaps the most spiritually capitalist moment in the game (at least as far as this book's argument is concerned) comes when players are challenged to answer this question, "WHAT RESOURCES DO YOU HAVE?" One worksheet accompanying the game lists conversation-starters such as "Skills & volunteers," "Your current activity," "What you are known for" "Buildings & spaces," etc. This is gamified spiritual capital: learning to re-see your life for its unlooked-for capital.

To make things even more wickedly challenging, once or twice throughout the contest, staff members would swirl among the tables announcing that a major crisis has just happened, that some of their resources have disappeared in a tornado or local flood. Groans would rise from around the room, adding to the room's cocktail of hilarity and anxiety. Eventually, the game culminates in a series of pitches for proposed problems and solutions. What I experienced on those game floors was not the affect I would ordinarily associate with any of the processes of social impact assessment. But the circuitry of feelings did suggest ways that old goods might move in new ways.

The inventors of the game from an organization called Rooted Good (formerly of Matryoshka Haus) offer this series of invitational questions to pull people like you into the game:

> What if you could play a game with a group of people that would help you imagine new ways to solve the complex problems you are working on? What if instead of holding another webinar with someone talking for an hour, you could engage your audience with an active workshop where everyone was involved and having fun? What if you could learn design thinking processes by playing a game instead of reading a book?[24]

Rooted Good turns the processes of impact design and assessment into a field of play through instruments like their "Mission Possible." Their website describes this activity as "a gamified workshop that helps organizations and innovators expand imagination and learn a design thinking process to solve big problems. By playing this physical or online game, teams build capacity to solve problems in their own context."[25] Rooted Good has numerous other exercises: they offer the What Now? toolkit for congregations and other sorts of organizations to deal with constraints and locate possibilities in a time of pandemic, as well as the Three Little Pigs Evaluation

24. Rooted Good, email message to author.
25. "Rooted Good," Rooted Good.

Exercise, the Community Discovery Tool, and the Transformation Index. These often-playful approaches to the processes of pursuing impact entail the peculiar removal-from-normality that a gameplayer almost always experiences. They also explicitly encourage organizations to look for perhaps obscure resources and unnoticed partners.

This approach to the question of achieving impact in a community is notably different than other standardized instruments now proliferating across the organizational impact space: Social Return on Investment (SROI); Impact Reporting and Investment Standards (IRIS); Social Accounting and Auditing (SAA); Cost-Benefit Analysis; and Balanced Scorecards. The affect of those tests is presumably fairly narrow—something like the feelings you'd have while taking a standardized test. But one such instrument that came up repeatedly in my interviews, the B Lab Assessment, unites the formality and rigor of a standardized test with the challenge and feel of a multi-player game.

The B Corp certification first appeared on a bag of King Arthur flour, soon after the B Lab opened in 2006. It did not take long for the B Corp certification to establish itself as a popular way for socially minded companies to certify their impact. Unlike some measures of impact, which assume that material change is elusive, the B Lab treated impact as something that every company brings about in some way or another. The challenge is quite simply to gauge "Positive Impact," by which the B Lab folks mean far more than compliance with federal regulations.[26] Even the test's extensive use of algorithmic design gives the feel of a game: as the website notes, "there are over 40 versions of the Assessment that are tailored to a company based on size (# of employees), sector, and geography."[27] Anybody can play, so long as they are willing to engage a cooperative, non-competitive gamification of assessment.

To achieve B Corp status requires strenuous effort. First, it entails attention to a broad range of organizational concerns: how an organization treats employees, how it engages their communities, how it relates to the natural world, how it manages customer relations, and how it pursues its mission. Although the B Corp certification uses the explicit language of assessment (it has to in order to persuade others of its reliability and rigor), it also uses a cheerful website aesthetic, pastel graphics, and score-taking to make impact assessment playful. Guiding companies through a highly structured set of queries, the B Lab Assessment invites a mode of engagement in which a company tries to score at least eighty points out of a possible two-hundred, which means that no company can win by doing well in just one area. But it is not at all the case that the B Lab folks set themselves up as the overlords

---

26. "What Makes the Assessment," B Impact Assessment.
27. "What Makes the Assessment," B Impact Assessment.

of certification; they actually invite participants to help them make their exercises better. They acknowledge that "the Assessment is far from being perfect, and it is possible that a significant change in the company is not perfectly correlated with the number of points earned. We would love your help on reweighting items that you feel should be worth more."[28]

So, that's the first affective infrastructure I've noticed among my interviewees, the gamification structure that they have sometimes produced for others and sometimes engaged in themselves. But this mode works with undeniably emotional power because it invites immersive enjoyment. The games create a good kind of detachment from everyday busyness and allow people to exercise skillful and imaginative problem-solving. Two potential shortcomings occur. Although organizations are compelled by these gamifications to think from their neighborhood's standpoint, they didn't (at least in the examples I cited) often enough invite neighbors to play the game with organizational members. Another shortcoming is that this mode invites hierarchical thinking. The collective playfulness and enjoyment that accompany gamification tend to be competitive. Although assessments like the B Lab talk about being "best for the world," not best *in* the world, humans are (as Kenneth Burke said long ago) "goaded by a spirit of hierarchy" and "rotten with perfection."[29] Still, gamification could become an affective path-maker for workplaces and communities to circulate affections and resources.[30]

ENCOUNTER

Some organizational leaders I spoke with pursued impact by making spaces for diverse people to interact. Charlie Branda tries to do this among White and Black citizens on Sedgwick Avenue. Tim Brand says that Many Hands for Haiti hosts "impact trips" for North Americans to interact with Haitians, ultimately for the sake of "[t]ransforming together, to be love in action, in a broken world."[31] Amor Montes de Oca says of the work at the incubator 2112, "[W]e're connecting entities that should know of each other, should be aware of each other, should collaborate, should . . . at the very least know of each other."[32] This mode of engagement has a strong phenomenological bent: it aims to alter how the self experiences the other from the inside out. As Charlie says, societal change is slow to come because people are slow to

28. "My B Impact Score," B Impact Assessment.

29. Burke, *Language as Symbolic Action.*

30. I got the term "social technology" from Liedtka, "Why Design Thinking Works."

31. "Many Hands For Haiti," Many Hands for Haiti.

32. Montes de Oca, interview by author, April 5, 2019.

get to know others different from themselves. She concedes that "it's very reasonable for me to not want to walk down the street and get shot. It's reasonable for me to say, okay, I'm going to move to somewhere there's fewer people with guns . . . . There's nothing really wrong with that mindset, but that's basically how we get to so many of the problems we have right now."[33] But organizations like Art on Sedgwick exist in order to disabuse people of the notion that a problem doesn't exist if you can't see it—or won't see it. "They pretend it doesn't happen, because they're living off in their little world where it doesn't impact them. That doesn't really solve the problem." Engaging this mode almost always entails entering dialogue between the self and the other. The rhythm of the mode entails that you hold onto your core identity while being open to embracing someone else's.

Here's another social entrepreneur who has made use of the mode of encounter to put new feelings and old goods into circulation. When Kendra Foley met me on a sunny, wintry day in a little teashop next to the School of the Art Institute Chicago (SAIC) on Wabash Avenue, she had just completed a successful $50,000 campaign. As a twenty-five-year veteran of the world of nonprofit fundraising, Kendra is well-acquainted with the exhaustion that comes at the end of a capital campaign. But at the time of our interview, Kendra was experimenting with another approach to capital through a social enterprise called Make Work. This project, she noted, has "turned into something that I never anticipated when I started it, which is actually informing all of my thinking around just everything."[34] What distinguished Make Work was not simply that it obtained new sources of revenue, as in, *We used to depend on donors, now we rely on enterprise.* In fact, Kendra expressed doubts about that way of thinking. "I think the more I learn about business, the harder it is to understand how business can solve all our problems."[35] But one thing a social enterprise can do is to create intensely interpersonal, perspective-changing encounters in its neighborhood

SAIC's board is peopled by wealthy patrons somewhat segregated from SAIC's students. The art students have low enough incomes that they rarely come to think of themselves as anything but the beneficiaries of the School. "They're used to being on the receiving end," Kendra explained. "They're used to being supported through grants. They're used to being supported through individuals who love them and work with development officers to

33. Branda, interview by author, June 28, 2019.
34. Foley, interview by author, February 13, 2019.
35. Foley, interview by author, February 13, 2019.

get them the professorship." Kendra asked herself the big impact question: "So how do we flip that?"[36]

Her work triggered a mode of engagement allowing for multidirectional, even multisectoral transformation in the neighborhoods of art and business. She began curating encounters between business mentors and student artists. The businesspeople tended to think that the artists were exotic and impractical; the artists tended to think that the business folk were soulless and uncultured. Kendra intensified the mode of encounter by asking mentors to donate $1000 to the school. From the perspective of the input-output-outcome value chain, this arrangement was nonsensical, a confusion of categories: she was treating an output as an input. But she wanted the business mentors not just to change their minds about artists—i.e., seeing them as really quite practical people after all—but rather to see how the worlds of business enterprise and artistic production are mutually entangled in inequitable systems.

Let me share one more instance of encounter being used as an approach to making possible new kinds of feelings and new kinds of circulation. Matt Overton told me about a conundrum he had faced some years previously as a youth minister. Although the paradigmatic approach to youth groups is event-planning—game nights and concerts and Bible studies and so on—he had discovered that some of his lower-income attenders had been put off by mingling with their wealthier counterparts, which, in turn, kept Matt from being able to pastor and mentor them as he felt called to do. "So, I was, like, how do I keep relationship with them? And then even from my high-performing kids that I wouldn't see, I was like, how am I going to keep relationship? There's so many activities. So I'm like, well, I bet if we pay them they would show up."[37] What he did was, in effect, to set aside the overt pastoral dimensions of his work in order to launch several businesses under one brand, the Columbia Future Forge. The incubational structure his enterprises created enabled him to mentor teenagers in ways that no youth group event could have simulated. "The image I use a lot," he explained, "is I think they feel like they've been asked to assemble a 1000-piece puzzle without the box, the picture on the box. And as anyone can tell you, that's hard to do. And so, part of my program was, through relationship, providing them more puzzle pieces, so they felt less anxiety and fear over stepping into the adult world."[38]

36. Foley, interview by author, February 13, 2019.

37. Overton, interview by author, October 25, 2019.

38. Overton, interview by author, October 25, 2019.

Organizational leaders and teams who practice this mode of encounter in order to engage their communities will find that it requires extensive skills: a feel for the cadence of listening and question-asking, a knack for evocative language and story, and a sometimes exquisite sense of timing. But those willing to cultivate artfulness can hope for the generation and circulation of new feelings in a community: empathy, fellow-feeling, compassion, startlement. Granted, the feelings generated by dialogue do have their limitations. As Peters has noted, we often exaggerate the efficacy of dialogue as a way to gain access to each other's souls.[39] But the mode of encounter need not be overbearing or unduly optimistic, especially if both parties recognize the perpetual need to constantly improvise these encounters.[40]

CHURCH

I expect my title for this style of engagement may raise a few eyebrows. Although my interviewees were often frustrated with, if not dismissive of, institutionalized faith, I learned to call this mode *church* from an atheist, who described herself as neither religious nor spiritual. Emily Lonigro described a warmhearted fellowship she holds with women professionals on a regular basis. "So, we drink, we eat junk food, and sometimes vegetables, and it's very low-key. It's at my house, and we set intentions. We talk about all of our stuff. Everybody cries almost every time. We stay till about midnight or 1:00 in the morning, and we just get it all out in a very secure, safe, brave environment that has a lockdown on—nothing leaves it."[41] And, she explained, "We call it church." But in many ways, companies like Emily's Lime Red Studio function like churches, or least as churches ought to be, in that they cultivate diverse memberships of people who wouldn't ordinarily find themselves in each other's company. They cultivate fellowship amongst themselves and with people outside the organization through shared meals, shared workspaces, and personal conversations one doesn't usually associate with professional life. They convey a congenially utopian view that organizations and their neighborhoods can enjoy beautiful community.

Tyler Etters and Jon Berbaum at Highland Solutions in our multiple interviews gave me a strong sense of this churchly mode. Before taking leadership at Highland, Jon had left the pastorate out of a sense of frustration with the power struggles in his denomination and now presides over

---

39. Peters, *Speaking into the Air,* 29–31.

40. In doing so, they also show what one sociologist calls "the strength of weak ties." Granovetter, "The Strength of Weak Ties," 1360–80.

41. Lonigro, interview by author, January 25, 2019.

this user-experience company. But he describes quasi-ecclesial dynamics in Highland's "mashup of people who are really wonderful together that our normal social categories would tell us should not be great together, right?"[42] He noted that even his collegiality, as a Christian, with Tyler, as an atheist, was a little unusual, adding that the company as a whole keeps close working relationships alive among people of faith and people in the LGBTQ community. "Normally, you'd be like, okay, let's talk about ourselves as little as possible so those two groups can get along. And that's not the way we've gone about it."[43] To protect that fellowship, Jon was willing to say no to a profitable client out of fear that the client's unhealth would poison Highland's fellowship. Tyler used similar membership language in speaking of how people could "join" their company "because you believe in the values, you believe in the people, you believe in the company we're trying to build." But this brings with it, he recognized, a responsibility to guard the health of the workplace. Tyler suggested, for example, that "part of our duty to you is to protect that and honor that agreement and keep you in healthy environments with our clients."[44] Like Emily, Jon and Tyler both told stories about clients they decided to turn down, on the grounds that the client would spread toxins in the Highland community or because the client espoused values counter to their social vision:

> We won the business for our company, and then we later found out that they sell firearms. And as a company, we decided that we didn't want to work with them on that. And that was a tough conversation. We went through the whole sales cycle, we talked about it. A lot of us believe the second amendment, all that stuff, but ultimately it's like, no this isn't aligned with the world that we're trying to build, and we had to say no.[45]

These, let's call them, sectarian difficulties made participation in this mode a matter of learning the cadence of what Miroslav Volf would call exclusion and embrace.[46]

Angie Thurston's incubator, the Sacred Design Lab, cultivates another ecclesial sort of fellowship, but across time and tradition. Impressed by the loneliness of professionals today, Angie attempts to help those separated from institutional religion by connecting them to the deep wisdom of sundry religious traditions. Without such wisdom, Americans tend, she

---

42. Berbaum, interview by author, June 13, 2019.
43. Berbaum, interview by author, June 13, 2019.
44. Etters, interview by author, April 12, 2019.
45. Etters, interview by author, April 12, 2019.
46. I draw this term from a book by that title: Volf, *Exclusion and Embrace*.

says, to reach out to all sorts of improbable spiritual experts: "A lot of my work has been in exploring sites of deep community outside of religion, whether it's fitness communities or gaming communities or maker spaces or justice movement or all this, and that's one piece of it."[47] To address these spiritual lacunae, Angie along with her colleagues Casper ter Kuile and Sue Phillips have launched the Sacred Design Lab to help companies cultivate the spiritual wellbeing of their employees. Because more and more people are looking for transcendence at work, company administrators find themselves short of the kind of spiritual know-how one would associate with a seminary education and theological training. An article in the *New York Times*, announced, "God Is Dead. So Is the Office. These People Want to Save Both."[48] The work of the Sacred Design Lab can be a little disconcerting for people who already inhabit deep faith traditions, especially because Angie and her colleagues "blend the obscure language of the sacred with the also obscure language of management consulting to provide clients with a range of spiritually inflected services, from architecture to employee training to ritual design."[49] But Angie, who describes herself as a "spiritual nerd," is trying to cultivate a certain spiritual virtuosity, connecting people, via long spreadsheet columns of spiritual practices, to faith traditions whose establishment presence has broken down—and then releasing them towards hoped-for spiritual wellbeing. She cultivates highly provisional fellowship with past religious voices.[50]

Just as religious vocation sometimes summons people who haven't initially felt qualified or even inclined to the work, social business calls some seemingly unlikely pastoral candidates, so to speak. Corey Kohn admitted that at one time, she would have repudiated business as a hopelessly compromised space. "I was in creative industries, mostly in film and photography . . . I was really much more interested in expression than in commerce. And I had no interest basically—and almost like this sense of revulsion against business—I think, because, number one, I didn't really understand it, and, number two, I think I had this sense that it's not about humans."[51] But now, helping to run DOJO4 in Boulder, Colorado provides her with a profound sense of community belonging. For a good decade, they've been hosting a Friday luncheon: "We do a little gathering beforehand, where we ask a question that's sometimes humorous, sometimes profound. We each

---

47. Thurston, interview by author, April 19, 2019.
48. Bowles, "God Is Dead."
49. Bowles, "God Is Dead."
50. Mattson, "The Island Only Feels Deserted—Angie Thurston."
51. Mattson, "It's about the Humans—Corey Kohn."

have a chance to answer if we want. It actually feels like, when I read about impact companies, the thing that often comes to my mind is that's probably more—the community we've created is probably more impactful than any of the work product that we do."[52]

This warmhearted mode obliges artfulness, tact, and, sometimes, silly good humor, a set of feelings that we might sum up as conviviality. Such feelings, however, are unavoidably clustered with feelings of dislike or even repulsion for people whose norms counter the churchly fellowship of an organization. I have mentioned in an earlier chapter how Corey's company worked exclusively with conscious clients, but then decided to broaden external partnerships. Angie's organization makes similarly broadening moves, threading together Buddhist, Christian and Confucian wisdoms for the improvement of workplace community. Other companies have instead narrowed their engagements. Conviviality can, by way of the dance of exclusion and embrace, move towards a tribalism already too common in American society.

GIFT

Jeff Melnyk and I talked about organizational spirituality over breakfast. As he eyed my smartphone PowerPoint slide of spiritual practices, he took a bite of mushrooms and then said, "I really wish—when we created the values for our business, I wish that there was a fifth value, and I wish that that value was generosity."[53] Many of my interviewees were similarly enthusiastic about giving as a way to conceptualize their work. Tiffany Hinton spoke of self-expansion "by giving of my love, joy, and abundance" to the point that such liberality is "overflowing out of me like a river."[54] Other people like Adam Melnyk (no relation to Jeff) felt quite strongly that generosity deprived beneficiaries of dignity. "I think that in the social entrepreneurship space," he explained, "the businesses that are the truly successful ones are the ones that are incorporating purpose, not out of a sense of generosity, but out of a sense that—"[55] Here Adam broke off for a moment, struggling for the right formulation. He seemed to recognize that the reciprocal mode he was trying to name, in some ways, countered mainstream economic thinking. "So, it's not about generosity. It's about, as a business owner, you still want to make as much money as you possibly can. You still want to have an

52. Kohn, interview by author, May 10, 2019.
53. Jeff Melnyk, interview by author, April 12, 2019.
54. Hinton, interview by author, March 31, 2019.
55. Adam Melnyk, interview by author, June 6, 2019.

incredibly vibrant, sustainable, successful business. You just are also trying to achieve something in a world that is in addition to that."[56] The important thing to do, these people would say, is not to give but to empower. It is not poverty that is the problem, they would explain, but dependence.

So, here is the puzzle: among the people I spoke with who were doing work in disadvantaged neighborhoods, generosity was often a prominent value. DeAmon Harges went around gathering stories of how his neighbors were giving money to each other without expecting return. Charlie Branda tied generosity closely with the vulnerability that inter-racial neighboring requires: "There's a generosity of spirit, which to me is part of forgiveness and mercy. I see that people aren't perfect, and I see myself as imperfect. I'm going to be kind and merciful to myself. What we offer to ourselves, we offer to other people. And then we can offer it to other people as well."[57] Pastah J talked about generosity in terms of risk-taking and supporting the risk-takers in Englewood:

> I really think that pastors, especially, and priests and imams, whoever else, should all be the ones pushing people towards entrepreneurship. Because we have an inherent belief in risk. I'm thinking this now, but it makes a lot of sense to me. We should be the ones pushing people out there to say, "Hey, not only do we believe because we believe, we believe in you because we believe, but there's a whole congregation and system that's here behind you that's gonna hopefully be there to support you."[58]

Often, the people promoting generosity seemed to be affirming an "extra" in human interaction that enables humane practice even in the apparently depersonalizing world of business exchange. The reason they had gotten into social business in the first place was to acknowledge and to celebrate with others what they liked to call a *mindset of abundance*, which they often contrasted with a *scarcity mindset*. For them, generosity was not so much a way to get things done as a way to say with others, *Isn't it great the world is this way, that it allows such ample community?*

On the other hand, those who opposed generosity discourse tended to celebrate reciprocity, giving pride of place to fairness and respect. Sarah Woolsey had gone into the social enterprise space because she was uneasy about "the kind of the toxic charity idea the church has." She quickly added that the church was hardly alone in this tendency towards paternalism. North Americans in general have "somehow distorted generosity a little bit

---

56. Adam Melnyk, interview by author, June 6, 2019.
57. Branda, interview by author, June 28, 2019.
58. Brooks, interview by author, May 22, 2019.

to feel top down in a lot of regards."[59] Robert White noted, in a similar vein that sometimes when people hear about his vocation at Cara, they'll say things like "that must help you sleep well at night—almost as if I'm just doing this out of the goodness of my heart." Robert objects to the notion, first, that his work is what enables him to sleep with an easy conscience, which "implies that I'm not doing anything in the rest of my life to be a good person, to be spiritually grounded, to interact and live my life in an intentional way." Like Adam, he wrestled with how to articulate this vocational complexity: "I guess that, I didn't want to be put in a camp of people who just said . . . 'You're being, you've chosen to be, self-sacrificing in some way, so that you can give, and that giving allows you to rest easy, because you're doing good work, or you're doing the Lord's work, or you're doing something that's somehow transcends day-to-day commerce. And I just don't think that's the reality of it. Because it's still work. I don't get paid to volunteer somewhere."[60]

Should these proponents and critics of generosity be lumped into the same mode of engagement? I believe so. As theologian Stephen Webb has argued at length, gifts are sometimes construed as excessive unilateral actions: a person gives, in other words, out of a sense of personal surplus and strength. That sort of giving could easily become paternalistic. On the other hand, the reciprocal exchange, which so wonderfully creates ongoing relationship, could easily reduce to a transactional arrangement. But Webb's theological argument grounds a conception of gift in the Christian doctrine of the Trinity's eternal exchange of excessive love. So, for Webb, generosity exchanges *and* surprises. Such a theology of gift, then, makes this mode encompass both those who emphasize exchange and those who emphasize the surplus.[61] The gift thus creates exuberant pathways for resource circulation thanks to the joyous feelings that so often accompany gift.

VIRTUOSITY

You remember Bryan Ungard of the tiger-eye bracelets, right? As we chatted, he tossed off an incidental remark that proved hard to forget: the ubiquitous term *impact*, he said, was starting to sound strange to him. "Sounds violent," he added.[62] I'm sure I jotted a note about this, because a later memory of

59. Woolsey, interview by author, March 27, 2019.

60. White, interview by author, January 23, 2019.

61. This is a summation of the argument Webb makes throughout his book *The Gifting God*.

62. Ungard, interview by author, April 12, 2019.

his comment provoked an etymological dig: I found that the term *impact* had entered the English language some 500 years ago, its oldest recorded use being adjectival. It meant something like the condition of being jammed in together, as in an impacted tooth. The term was picked up around the same time by physicists to describe "the act of impinging; the striking of one body against another; collision."[63] Impact does, come to think of it, sound like a crater site. Little wonder, then, that when we're trying to manage such a huge event, we reach for a manageable metaphor, the impact value chain.

But after spending time examining the four organizational styles described in this chapter, I wonder about exchanging the metaphor of the impact chain for the image of a prayer labyrinth, a series of meandering but concentric paths often used by people for contemplative practice. The work of running a company for the betterment of external partners and adjacent communities asks, I think, for artfulness—like that required to make a labyrinth. There's something mischievous about these pathways, which take you inwards till you think you've almost arrived and then suddenly move you all the way to the outer ring. But they have an apt amount of order and enigma, so that people in the same labyrinth meet, going and coming, some wending toward the center of organizational wellbeing and some heading outwards to the community's wellbeing.

I think that's one of the big findings of this final chapter, that sharing feelings takes a surprising skillfulness and imagination. It's hard not to think of feelings as events that just happen, like moods or obsessions. But making feelings collective, especially in playful, joyous, convivial spaces like these organizations have created, entails virtuosity. Just as a smart Tweet or an apt Instagram post or a deft podcast question requires skill, so these modes of Gamification, Church, Encounter, and Gift each require and coach participants in adeptness.

That adroitness reminds me of something Corey Kohn once said about impact, when she suggested that "doing meaningful work, whatever the content of the work is, having the work feel meaningful, is actually the most powerful in terms of personal and societal impact." As an example, she talked about work DOJO4 has done for Twitter, hardly an aspirational company. But the work has nonetheless given her employees challenging, interesting code to make. "When people come to work, they're excited about the work they're doing, and they don't feel like they're just creating some stupid thing."[64] Tyler Etters at Highland Solutions talked about how an ethic of doing good work shapes his organizational life and leadership:

63. "Impact," Oxford English Dictionary Online. Accessed December 20, 2020.
64. Kohn, interview by author, May 10, 2019.

Even if no other human will ever see it, it matters. Even if only you see it, it matters. Because you know the next time you use it or when you pass it on to someone, that it was created with that degree of care. So, I extend that to my work . . . but it manifests in a lot of ways. Sometimes it's just taking a minute to offer comfort to a fellow teammate, to extend care, compassion to a client.[65]

That sort of art and skill and imagination simply in the doing of worthwhile work suggests a way to encapsulate the collective emotions this chapter has discussed. We might speak of enjoyment and conviviality and empathy and surprise under the tab of virtuosity.[66]

"Whatever your hand finds to do," writes Qoheleth, "do it with all your might; for there is no work or thought or knowledge or wisdom in Sheol, to which you are going."[67] Life is brief, he seems to be saying, so do your living and working with virtuosity. In the same passage, he appends a phrase with what Ellen Davis calls "remarkable incautiousness."[68] After calling us to enjoyment, Qoheleth says, "for God has long ago approved what you do."[69] Davis suggests, "God likes the way you fulfil your responsibilities, even the way you meet your basic necessities, including the necessity of companionship. Such an assurance could be healing for us, who habitually engage in excess."[70] It is striking, in a book remembered for its cynicism, how numerous are Qoheleth's calls to joy. Rejoice in your work, he says. Rejoice in your friends and relations. Rejoice in food and sleep. Rejoice in sunlight. Rejoice in every year of life you are given. Davis notes, "One might think that we who live in a hedonistic society do not need to be told to enjoy ourselves. But perhaps the problem is that we do not *sufficiently* enjoy the means by which we obtain our necessities and the small luxuries that ordinary life affords."[71]

How to cultivate sufficient enjoyment of work in community? Counter to the earnest optimism of so many theories of change, this chapter's organizational modes show what becomes circulatable when unserious feelings circulate. Given the severity of the world's predicaments, are feelings such as

---

65. Etters, interview by author, April 12, 2019.

66. I draw this term from Berry whose discussion of the Great Economy has consistently informed my own thinking about spirituality capital as a way to access to other forms of capital as well. See Berry, *What Matters*, 135.

67. Ecclesiastes 9:10 NRSV.

68. Davis, *Proverbs, Ecclesiastes, and Song of Songs*, 213.

69. Ecclesiastes 9:7 NRSV.

70. Davis, *Proverbs, Ecclesiastes, and Song of Songs*, 214.

71. Davis, *Proverbs, Ecclesiastes, and Song of Songs*, 214.

hilarity and playfulness and conviviality and happy surprise really suitable? "I have seen the business that God has given to everyone to be busy with," Qoheleth might say, "He has made everything suitable for its time."[72] Discerning that suitability, that aptness, is a great part of virtuosic living. Davis notes that the fragility and fleetingness of our experiences suggest that living well is "not a matter of good luck but a work of great delicacy and skill."[73] Virtuosity entails discerning what time it is. This skill in the art of being human constantly confronts us with what Davis calls "a crucial element of choice:" "We must decide whether our posture will be one of acceptance or resistance, whether we will fight to the death the ever-changing rhythms of life, or whether we will dance to them."[74]

Perhaps we should change the "impact" tabs on organizational websites to "virtuosity" tabs. It is, after all, the good feelings that circulate in virtuosic labor which channel once-hidden resources towards community. These are resources made collectively accessible along the labyrinthine pathways of shared feeling. As I write these final sentences, I imagine these interview subjects shaking their heads gently at the way I have tucked their varied organizations into a single mode. They would be right so to complain. Although their organizations and communities tended to prefer one affective route over another, they often used more than one. Perhaps their final wisdom for us, then, is that a plurality of shareable affections is the best index of spiritual capital.[75]

---

72. Ecclesiastes 3:10–11 NRSV.

73. Davis, Proverbs, Ecclesiastes, and Song of Songs, 184.

74. Davis, Proverbs, Ecclesiastes, and Song of Songs, 184.

75. I am indebted to Jenkins's discussions of modes, affect, and circulation for this discussion of ways of interfacing. See Jenkins, "The Modes of Visual Rhetoric," 442–66.

Afterword

THESE PAST SIX CHAPTERS have used a spiritual capital lens to trace the movements of social and economic capital within organizations and within their neighborhoods. But how should organizational leaders and their teams cultivate the capital needed to see and circulate such subtle goods, such latent resources? I'd like to propose in this final word some practical guidance for the peculiar accounting required by spiritual capital investments.

The most vital place to start would be with how leaders and their colleagues imagine the self in relation to the other. When I do a quick index of my own imaginations for such encounters, I find I resort to several analogies developed by prominent thinkers and writers. Perhaps the following are pictures that help guide your organizational imagination as well:

Think first of the Narrow Ridge: Martin Buber has helped envision a way of living with others that does not amble companionably around the sunny meadows of an utterly familiar system of thought, where everything connects to everything else, and where any part of the meadow is reachable from any other part. Instead, he envisions a ledge, jagged and narrow, with an abyss on each side. People traverse the ledge delicately but courageously hopeful of encounter. For Buber, the one abyss might be the "I" who I so mysteriously am, while the other side is the "Thou" who you so wondrously are. The point is not to find balance, but to maintain a reverent tension.[1]

Or take, the Country Dance. Anne Morrow Lindbergh envisions a marriage as rhythmed, cadenced, moved by periods of togetherness, seasons of apartness, much as two dancers draw together at certain points in a quadrille, but without clinging to one another. In a later movement of the same dance, they may be moving away from one another or stepping in

---

1. Discussion of the narrow ridge can be found in Buber, *Between Man and Man*. The dynamics of this relationship can be explored in Buber, *I and Thou*.

time but facing outwardly. "Now arm in arm, now face to face, now back to back—it does not matter which," writes Lindbergh. "Because they know they are partners moving to the same rhythm, creating a pattern together, and being invisibly nourished by it."[2]

Finally, consider the picture of the Embrace, Miroslav Volf's metaphor for an encounter between two parties, not in terms of unknowability or rhythms, but in terms of respectful affection. For him, the self and the other come together in a series of ethical moments. First, one of the selves opens her arms. This is an invitation, not a demand, which entails that, in the second moment, the self awaits response. If the invitee is amenable, then the third moment, the coming-together in a hug, can happen. But the final moment of the embrace obliges a letting-go, a release, lest the embrace become oppressive.[3]

In any case, it would be worth time in your organizational life to think aloud together about how you both imagine your workplace neighborhood and how you actually live these pictures out. What figures, what rhythms, what stories shape the pictures in your heads for good encounter? Those pictures will further shape how you enable and sometimes constrain the discernment and circulation of subtle goods in your workplace and its neighborhood.

But if you want to take this a funny and illumining step further, you should throw a White Elephant Gift Party. Stay with me. I will concede that my proposal is animated by the fact that I write this on the eve of Christmas Eve, 2020. But I believe organizational leaders and their teams need a fresh way to dramatize the complex and communal movements described in previous chapters. Our imaginations, like the analogies suggested above, are often vivid, warmhearted, and spiritually infused. But they are also relentlessly dyadic. They reduce all too often to twosomes, not to the nimble circulations of community envisioned in the previous chapter. Hence, my proposal to try an undignified way of introducing a working community to spiritual capital: the White Elephant Gift Exchange.

You probably know some version of the following rules:

1. Each person must bring a present—silly, odd, or desirable, it doesn't matter too much, so long as it is not too expensive—and then plop that gift into the communal pile.

---

2. Lindbergh, *Gift from the Sea*, 104.

3. Volf, *Exclusion and Embrace*, 99–166.

2. The participants circle up around the pile and, after randomly selecting who goes first, someone selects an item, unwraps it, usually to the
   amusement or envy of everybody else present.

3. Person by person, then, each participant chooses either to take an
   already-opened gift from someone else's lap or to try their luck with
   the mysterious packages in the middle of the circle.

4. If the gift in your lap is absconded with by someone else, then you are
   freed to follow a similar procedure—either selecting someone else's
   gift or snatching one from the pile.

5. Usually, the circle of "Yankee Swappers" agrees that after a gift has
   been snatched three times from someone's clutches, then it must be
   taken out of circulation and left to the hands of the third (or is it the
   fourth?) person who enjoys its possession.

6. The game proceeds until every gift has either been circulated three
   times or taken and held uncontested.

What this sometimes dispiriting game of gifting helps us envision
about spiritual capital within a workplace community is a series of encounters among participants in that community, encounters that do not reduce
to a one-on-one interaction. The game works out sometimes obnoxious,
sometimes too-competitive, sometimes hilarious ways of being generous
together.

One gain in this activity is that in order for the game to be fun, we
have to rethink the concept and practice of goods, not as things to be held
on to, not as things to be donated to one other special person, but as things
to be kept in motion for as long as possible. There's a non-reciprocity to the
exchange that counters our usual expectations and can be playfully illumining. Let's say you had a crush on someone at work and you went shopping
for a gift for them in particular; your gift still gets thrown into the White
Elephant pile and the romantic aims are thwarted. At the same time, new,
surprising relations open up. And, who knows, perhaps by dint of inadver-
tent collaboration, by no means under your control, that gift ends up in the
hands of the person you admire after all. You can't take credit for the arrival
of the goods in their hands. At the same time, you were thoroughly invested
in the process that brought it about.

But there are other ways this game tutors a working community in
spiritual capital. The suggestion of an "elephant" points to new possibilities
of scale within our community's circulation. Customarily, gift-giving is a
delicate thing at precisely this point. If I give a birthday present that is too
extravagant—a brand new Audi—you might be impressed, but also anxious

about the sheer size of the gift. Perhaps the gift seems out of proportion to our relationship: I'm your neighbor two doors down, for crying out loud, and we've spoken only once! Perhaps the oversized gift comes off as a self-aggrandizing bid to improve my status. But in a White Elephant Gift circle, extravagance is welcome. The scale of the weirdness makes the game all the more fun. The zanier the Christmas sweater, the better the gift performs. Even if you bring a recognizably expensive gift to the party, the recipient of the gift cannot accuse you of trying to impress her, because you cannot engineer the circulation, except perhaps indirectly. Put differently, learning to see with a spiritual capital lens entails developing an eye for incongruous goods, unexpected resources.

After you do your White Elephant exchange, I recommend discussing with your team how spiritual capital entails discernment of goods that are present but hidden, resources that are there but obscure. This kind of capital, in other words, activates other kinds of goods. Spiritual capital is for the better circulating of economic and social capital. Such capital, you could point out, moves community interactions out of the narrow confines of reciprocal exchange and into the wilder, more expansive circulations of a diverse community. And that takes some getting used to.

I have found help in Kenneth Burke's terminology of *perfection*. I have for years taught rhetoric students Burke's notion of how humans tend to push a way of speaking to its extremity in order to make a point or win an argument. Sometimes, Burke says, we become "rotten with perfection" by taking a terminology to an absurd and self-destructive point. This kind of conceptual purification gets worked out and lived out in a social practice of some sort or another. For example, the Manhattan Project scientists took the concepts of quantum physics to such a perfection point that they developed a weapon capable not just of defeating an enemy, but also of destroying the world of the bombmakers themselves. White supremacists take the good of community membership, but perfect it to the point of a horrible exclusivity through Jim Crow mandates and ultimately towards self-destructiveness as redlining and block-busting destroy the cities of those who originally sought to benefit from such exclusivity. Gradually, as the terminology and practice get refined, a community may purify itself of all the essential complications and indispensable extraneous elements that make up human life in community.

John M. Barclay, however, has appropriated the Burkean concept of perfection with a more benign vector. As a Christian theologian, Barclay notes that within the life of the Triune God there is an enactment of gift that is perfected without rottenness. Although Barclay has not worked out the social economics of this gift-perfection yet, his theology provides the beginnings of a schema for circulating mutuality in a working community. He identifies six kinds of perfection, some of which you will recognize as informing my discussion of White Elephant Gifts above:

1. Superabundance—the scale of the gift (extravagant proportions)

2. Singularity—the intentionality of the gift (pure aims)

3. Priority—the timing of the gift (unexpected arrival)

4. Incongruity—the conditionality of the gift (indiscriminate distribution)

5. Efficacy—the consequentiality of the gift (enabling action)

6. Non-circularity—the unilateral gift (gratuitous movement)[4]

These might also be seen as ways that spiritual capital enables a perfecting of other kinds of capital—that is, a lifting of economic and social goods out of dormancy (out of the White Elephant pile, so to speak) and moving them into vigorous, practical circulation in the community (like that Christmas Gnome who somehow keeps showing up on a different person's desk throughout the year). When it comes to the critical conversations that organizational leaders so often feel they must hold with colleagues, team members, and external partners, a spiritual capital mode shifts the script of those conversations.

Let's think through some of these scripts for a moment. With a colleague who has lost sight of the larger mission of the organization, for example, the administrator would usually say something like this,

> *I know that your work is very demanding. I can't tell you enough how grateful I am for what you do so well in this company. We ask you to do a lot around here, and you consistently deliver. But I also know how easy it is—believe me, I know this all too well!—to be so overwhelmed by all that you personally have to do that you lose sight of what we're all trying to do together. But I'd like to ask you to think about this from your coworker's perspective for a minute. Just this morning, one of your teammates came to me, complaining that you've been neglecting . . .*

And so forth and so on. The basic move is to identify with the predicament of the colleague, to show them that you see things from their perspective, that you comprehend their difficulties. And then, after establishing this identification and empathy, after showing that you stand on the same ground with the other, you invite her or him to practice a similar identification with another person, the irritated coworker.

4. Barclay, *Paul & the Gift*, 70–75.

This is a good and time-tested practice of empathetic conversation. It requires a great deal of tact and time, and if the coworker can get the hang of it from you, such conversation can reward the ethical labor by facilitating other good encounters across the company. Other narrow ridges can be traversed, other embraces enabled, other dances begun. That sort of dialogue seems all to the good.

But spiritual capital's cultivation requires a change in script. We need a way of speaking that gets at what we do not yet know together. In a dyad, we generally know, at least in a sense, who we're dealing with: you and me, the self and the other. But in this case, our community doesn't know its own boundaries yet, doesn't know who it can attach to and articulate with. We don't know the limits of the circulatory pathways. Nor do we know the "what" of our community's goods. And when it comes to our adjacent communities, the resources may be even less visible. This takes some getting used to, because we think we can usually quantify the resources in a given situation. Spiritual capital makes us be open to resources we have never noticed.

Let's say there's a disagreement about who's supposed to be doing what in your organization. (This is purely hypothetical, of course. You never have such conflicts on your team, but humor me.) The fact that somebody is complaining about a colleague's neglect of work suggests that this circle starts small—just two or three, perhaps. But the circle can expand at any point that such expansion would increase spiritual capital. The script for you, as the initiator of such a conversation might be something like this:

> *Right, so we could talk about this in terms of how we're distributing tasks. Actually, we will get to that conversation, and soon. But before we go there, let's ask a different sort of question. A different set of questions. Let's ask what would happen if we stopped worrying about her selfish intentions or his tendency to avoid work, if we stopped being anxious about getting our just deserts in each of our divisions. I think it's possible that what looks like somebody being lazy might be due to something we're all missing. Many things we're all missing. Maybe our colleague who's focused on one set of tasks and is ignoring others is doing so because she sees goods right in the midst of us that the rest of us are missing.*

This script could open room for discussing what has remained unnoticed as a resource in your workplace or its neighborhood because its scale is so huge. The script might also initiate new approaches to regular work. Instead of asking what's chronologically demanded by a customary deadline (*We have to get those reports in by the last week of the month*), this spiritual capital approach might ask what has become subtly seasonable, suddenly fitting in our midst.

The capability to recognize and activate these subtle goods entails a different sort of conversation: not one aiming at reconciling fixed and opposing standpoints (like the metaphors by Buber, Lindbergh, and Volf), but one aspiring to see the as-yet invisible. The aim is to make what's been overlooked fully apparent and then to pull that into relationships where the goods can be used to build wealth and wellbeing. The heedless colleague can be reimagined as someone paying extravagant attention to a resource whose hidden scale surprises everybody else when it becomes visible.

I experienced something like this White Elephant Party, even in the course of finishing up this manuscript. Social entrepreneurs, I have found, are dangerous people to be around, especially if like me you just want to keep your head down and produce your work on time. Their networking skills and their abrupt recognition of goods in unexpected places can pull a pedantic author like me right out of the regular grind of writing a thousand words a day, or whatever goal the writer sets, and into subtle networks. Even in the final weeks of writing this manuscript, I found myself drawn into a Neighborhood Economics project in south Chicago, dreamed up in conversations between Kevin Jones, a social impact investor and community engager, and Aaron Kuecker, the provost of the college where I teach. There is an enormous amount of joy in this expanding network. It feels zany, and more than once I have called up somebody in the network just to share the familiar reciprocal exchange of a joke about something strange that somebody else is doing. The more productive you are in a network like this, the funnier your actions become from a conventional perspective. But the gifts circulate and accelerate, managed by no one person in particular and involving an ever-expanding circle of participants—academics, economists, community organizers, pastors, coders, and social entrepreneurs.

The Neighborhood Economics group, peopled with folks from a dozen different vocational standpoints, seeks to keep economically squeezed people in their houses and in their neighborhoods, despite the frequent inequities of mortgage economics. What holds together a collaboration like this? Some days I'm not sure at all. But it's a White Elephant gift party, all right: the incongruities of the gifts that surface and circulate keep us all jumping and dreaming and thinking and, in my case, writing. Unlike the organization you yourself lead and work for, the Neighborhood Economics group has no brand, no infrastructure, no managerial office. But there is a rapid and energizing circulation that none of us feels like we started, a quick-moving recognition that generously economic possibilities are already present in the neighborhoods like Woodlawn and Englewood. I write these words out of conviction that other unlooked-for circulations are releasable in your company, your nonprofit, your congregation, your school.

When I lose my hold on how spiritual capital works, I find help in the poetry of David Whyte in collections like *Pilgrim*, and in poems such as "Thoor Anu," where he speaks of the blessed circulations of the goods of the world. He paints this interaction in massive and gorgeous fashion on a bluff in Scotland, overlooking the sea—the mysterious, overwhelming, gracious encounter of the human being with all that makes up the world. Human beings have materialized, have appeared, only briefly, which requires them to accept their own contingency.[5] It's a picture that evokes Qoheleth's casting of bread upon the water, awaiting its return after many days.

---

5. Whyte, *Pilgrim*.

Bibliography

Ahmed, Sara. *The Cultural Politics of Emotion*. New York: Routledge, 2004.

"All About Motivations at Cara." Cara. Accessed December 20, 2020. https://carachicago. org/about-motivations/.

Austin, J. L. *How to Do Things with Words*. 2nd ed. Cambridge: Harvard University Press, 1975.

Barclay, John. *Paul & the Gift*. Grand Rapids: Eerdmans, 2015.

Bartholomew, Craig. *Ecclesiastes*. Grand Rapids: Baker Academic, 2009.

Beaumont, Susan. *How to Lead When You Don't Know Where You're Going: Leading in a Liminal Season*. London: Rowman & Littlefield, 2019.

Berlant, Lauren. "Cruel Optimism." In *The Affect Theory Reader*, edited by Melissa Gregg and Gregory J. Seigworth. Durham: Duke University Press 2011.

Berry, Wendell. "An Argument for Diversity." *The Hudson Review* 42 (1990) 537–48.

———. "Sabbaths—1979, IV." In *A Timbered Choir*. Washington, DC: Counterpoint, 1998.

———. *What Matters?: Economics for a Renewed Commonwealth*. Berkeley: Counterpoint, 2010.

"Blake Mycoskie—Global Leadership Summit, 2010." YouTube video uploaded by wcavideo. April 12, 2012. http://www.youtube.com/watch?v=f5OCcD4qbk8.

Blumenthal, Neil. "Warby Parker's Neil Blumenthal: How We Turned $120,000 Into a Billion-Dollar Eyeglass Brand." Inc. Video. Accessed on July 5, 2017. https://www. inc.com/neil-blumenthal/how-we-built-a-billion-dollar-eyeglass-brand.html.

Bonhoeffer, Dietrich. *Letters & Papers from Prison*. New York: Touchstone, 1971.

Booth, Wayne. *The Rhetoric of Fiction*. Chicago: University of Chicago Press, 1961.

Bourdieu, Pierre. "The Forms of Capital." Originally published in 1986. Accessed 14 December 2020. https://www.marxists.org/reference/subject/philosophy/works/ fr/bourdieu-forms-capital.htm.

Bowles, Nellie. "God Is Dead. So Is the Office. These People Want to Save Both." *The New York Times*. August 28, 2020. https://www.nytimes.com/2020/08/28/business/ remote-work-spiritual-consultants.html?action=click&module=Editors%20 Picks&pgtype=Homepage.

Brand, Tim. *Transforming Together: How Love in Action Can Transform Our World*. Pella: Many Hands for Haiti, 2019.

Branda, Charlie. "Art Helps Diverse Neighbors Create A Shared Identity." TED: Ideas Worth Sharing. December 2019. https://www.ted.com/talks/charlie_branda_art_helps_diverse_neighbors_create_a_shared_identity.

Brown, Jonathan. "Ethical shopping: The Red Revolution." *The Independent.* January 27, 2006. https://www.independent.co.uk/news/world/politics/ethical-shopping-red-revolution-6110673.html.

Buber, Martin. *Between Man and Man.* Translated by Ronald Gregor Smith. London: Kegan Paul, 1947.

———. *I and Thou.* Translated by Ronald Gregor Smith. New York: Charles Scribner's Sons, 1958.

Burke, Kenneth. *Language as Symbolic Action: Essays on Life, Literature, and Method.* Berkeley: University of California Press, 1966.

Burton, Tara Isabella. *Strange Rites: New Religions for a Godless World.* New York: Hachette Book Group, 2020.

Cain, Susan. *Quiet: The Power of Introverts in a World That Can't Stop Talking.* New York: Crown, 2012.

Canfield, Jack, et al. *Chicken Soup for the Soul at Work.* Deerfield Beach: Backlist, 2012.

"Changing the World One Step at a Time." *CNN.* September 26, 2008. http://edition.cnn.com/2008/BUSINESS/09/26/mycoskie.interview/index.html.

Cole, Shawn, et al. "Background Note: Managing and Measuring Impact." Harvard Business School Background Note. April 18, 2018. https://www.hbs.edu/faculty/Pages/item.aspx?num=54418.

Condit, Celeste Michelle. *Angry Public Rhetorics: Global Relations and Emotion in the Wake of 9/11.* Ann Arbor: University of Michigan Press, 2018.

Connell, James, and Anne Kubisch. "Applying a Theory of Change Approach to the Evaluation of Comprehensive Community Initiatives: Progress, Prospects, and Problems." Washington, DC: Aspen Institute, 1998.

Crary, Jonathan. *24/7: Late Capitalism and the Ends of Sleep.* London: Verso, 2013.

———. *Suspensions of Perception: Attention, Spectacle, and Modern Culture.* Cambridge: MIT Press, 2001.

"Creating Inclusive High-Tech Incubators and Accelerators: Strategies to Increase Participation Rates of Women and Minority Entrepreneurs." JPMorgan Chase & Co. May 2016. https://www.jpmorganchase.com/content/dam/jpmc/jpmorgan-chase-and-co/documents/icic_jpmc_incubators_r7.pdf.

Davis, Ellen. *Proverbs, Ecclesiastes, and the Song of Songs.* Louisville: Westminster John Knox Press, 2000.

Deetz, Stanley, and Jennifer Simpson. "Critical Organizational Dialogue: Open Formation and the Demand of 'Otherness.'" In *Dialogue: Theorizing Difference in Communication Studies,* edited by Rob Anderson, et al. Thousand Oaks: Sage, 2004.

"DOJO4." DOJO4. Accessed December 20, 2020. https://dojo4.com/.

Easterly, William. T*he White Man's Burden: Why the West's Efforts to Aid the Rest Have Done So Much Ill and So Little Good.* New York: Penguin, 2007.

"Ed Whitfield: Creating a Culture for Economic Democracy." Youtube video uploaded by SOCAP Global. May 23, 2019. https://www.youtube.com/watch?v=cdSVHhKH4yA.

Eldson, Mark. *We Aren't Broke: Uncovering Hidden Resources for Mission and Ministry.* Grand Rapids: Eerdmans, 2021.

Enns, Peter. *Ecclesiastes*. Grand Rapids: Eerdmans, 2011.

Etters, Tyler. "How We Assign Team Members to Projects as a People-First Agency. It's called Tetris—and it's awesome." Highland Solutions. March 5, 2020. https://highlandsolutions.com/blog/how-we-assign-team-members-to-projects-as-a-people-first-agency.

Ford, David. *Christian Wisdom: Desiring God and Learning in Love*. Cambridge: Cambridge University Press, 2007.

———. *The Shape of Living: Spiritual Directions for Everyday Life*. Grand Rapids: Baker, 2004.

Fisher, Walter. *Human Communication as Narration: Toward a Philosophy of Reason, Value, and Action*. Columbia: University of South Carolina Press, 1989.

Gallagher, Winifred. *Rapt: Attention and the Focused Life*. New York. Penguin, 2009.

Giridharadas, Anand. *Winners Take All: The Elite Charade of Changing the World*. New York: Knopf, 2018.

Goleman, Daniel. *Focus: The Hidden Driver of Excellence*. New York: HarperCollins, 2013.

Godin, Seth. *This is Marketing*. New York: Portfolio/Penguin, 2018.

Granovetter, Mark S. "The Strength of Weak Ties." *American Journal of Sociology* 78 (1973) 1360–80. https://sociology.stanford.edu/sites/g/files/sbiybj9501/f/publications/the_strength_of_weak_ties_and_exch_w-gans.pdf.

Griffin, Em, et al. *A First Look at Communication Theory Conversations with Communication Theorists*. 9th ed. New York: McGraw-Hill, 2015.

Harris, Malcolm. *Kids These Days: Human Capital and the Making of Millennials*. New York: Little, Brown and Company, 2017.

Hardt, Michael. "Affective Labor." *Boundary 2* 26 (1999) 89–100. Accessed December 21, 2020. http://www.jstor.org/stable/303793.

Healy, Jack, et al. "'The weapon that will end the war': Vaccinations begin across virus-ravaged America." *The New York Times*. Dec. 18, 2020. https://www.nytimes.com/live/2020/12/14/world/covid-19-coronavirus.

"Highland." Highland Solutions. Accessed December 20, 2020. https://highlandsolutions.com/.

"Home." Parity Homes. Accessed December 20, 2020. https://www.parityhomes.com/.

Hopkins, Shannon. "Shannon Hopkins: How to Lead When Things Are Falling Apart." *Faith & Leadership*. July 21, 2020. https://faithandleadership.com/shannon-hopkins-how-lead-when-things-are-falling-apart.

Huber, Lindsay Perez. "Challenging Racist Nativist Framing: Acknowledging the Community Cultural Wealth of Undocumented Chicana College Students to Reframe the Immigration Debate." *Harvard Educational Review* 79 (2009) 704–30. https://pdfs.semanticscholar.org/1dc3/a82326dfbed145f30cc42cd879fde1fd21c3.pdf.

Jackson, Maggie. *Distracted: The Erosion of Attention and the Coming Dark Age*. New York: Prometheus, 2009.

Jenkins, Eric. "The Modes of Visual Rhetoric: Circulating Memes as Expressions." *Quarterly Journal of Speech* 100 (2014) 442–66.

"Join(RED)." Join(RED). Internet Archive Wayback Machine. April 18, 2010. http://web.archive.org/web/20100418215849/http://www.joinred.com/aboutred.

Jolly, Jasper. "SoftBank boss takes blame for £5bn loss after WeWork punt." *The Guardian.* November 6, 2019. https://www.theguardian.com/business/2019/nov/06/japanese-tech-investor-softbank-hit-by-huge-quarterly-loss-wework-uber.

Keeley-Jonker, Bethany. "The Virtual Body of Christ in a Suffering World." *Christian Scholar's Review* 47 (2018) 305–7.

Kim, Young, II, writer. *Billions.* Season 1, episode 4, "Short Squeeze." Directed by James Foley. Aired February 7, 2016. Best Available! TBTF Productions Inc., 2016.

Konnikova, Maria. *Mastermind: How to Think like Sherlock Holmes.* New York: Penguin, 2013.

Laird, Martin. *An Ocean of Light: Contemplation, Transformation, and Liberation.* New York: Oxford, 2019.

Lanham, Richard. *The Economics of Attention: Style and Substance in the Age of Information.* Chicago: University of Chicago Press, 2006.

Latour, Bruno. *Reassembling the Social: An Introduction to Actor-Network Theory.* Oxford: Oxford University Press, 2005.

Liedtka, Jeanne. "Why Design Thinking Works." *Harvard Business Review.* September–October, 2018. https://hbr.org/2018/09/why-design-thinking-works.

Lindbergh, Anne Morrow. *Gift from the Sea.* New York: Pantheon, 1955.

MacIntyre, Alasdair. *After Virtue.* Notre Dame: University of Notre Dame Press, 1981.

Mackie, Tim, and Jon Collins. "Wisdom Series: Proverbs." *The BibleProject Podcast.* Podcast audio. June 8, 2016. https://bibleproject.com/podcast/wisdom-series-proverbs.

"Many Hands For Haiti–Transforming Together." Many Hands for Haiti. Accessed December 15, 2020. https://www.mh4h.org/.

Mattson, Craig. "Buying Stuff. Saving Lives—A Critical Account of Product RED's Economics of Attention." *Southern Journal of Communication* 77 (2012) 216–38.

———. "Good Grief and Organizational Change—Shannon Hopkins." *Spiritual Capital.* Podcast audio. August 13, 2020. https://open.spotify.com/episode/1jk670 3Y8eOF04Q7sOsGgy?si=PGMWdD31T6Kf-ifxvyPOPQ.

———. "Household Economics at Highland Solutions—Jon Berbaum." *Spiritual Capital.* Podcast audio. December 11, 2020. https://open.spotify.com/episode/4J DiaQGsvvIy2342mDA9yO?si=KMVq2aYLR6CsmW8v94d4eg.

———. "The Island Only Feels Deserted—Angie Thurston." *Spiritual Capital.* Podcast audio. September 24, 2020. https://open.spotify.com/episode/2vbVJhgZINWotfE aNdhLOh?si=2l1XvxD3TsmOz5BmvZU3AQ.

———. "It's about the Humans—Corey Kohn." *Spiritual Capital.* Podcast audio. July 24, 2020. https://open.spotify.com/episode/4ZJTIlSDwCt2QtjBuUnJ5A?si=rUO oq9QnTr-PIU-ruaCTfQ.

———. "Kohlrabi Capital—Janelle St. John." *Spiritual Capital.* Podcast audio. October 8, 2020. https://open.spotify.com/episode/6pxzoOjtNtBDSc2nbfafTV?si=gcL73jg LTouP39TruHvXAQ.

———. "Nothing about Us without Us—Patrick Reyes." *Spiritual Capital.* Podcast audio. July 10, 2020. https://open.spotify.com/episode/2QXLdJCbAbxz2kRvKoO 9CJ?si=qJEnRKFmQleo_DcqC9TpgA.

———. "On Roving & Listening in a Pandemic—DeAmon Harges." *Spiritual Capital.* Podcast audio. April 16, 2020. https://open.spotify.com/episode/1KIfLArhvjELP QUQhlbuF5?si=fv6Q6_l8SMuc1ABe-9XDpA.

————. "Reclaiming the Hood—Devonta Boston." *Spiritual Capital*. Podcast audio. August 20, 2020. https://open.spotify.com/episode/1vs4kcCoZpzOVoKMhJJZs2? si=paTEwDNVQl6qW4Ophhs79Q.

————. *Rethinking Communication in Social Business: How Re-Modeling Communication Keeps Companies Social and Entrepreneurial*. Lanham: Lexington, 2018.

————. "The Spirit in the Details—Emily Lonigro." *Spiritual Capital*. Podcast audio. August 28, 2020. https://open.spotify.com/episode/56r7PuVG2GHyfgIaUzxZzm ?si=eTm_DbvpTxqH_1CXrFYoqQ.

————. "Telling the Neighborhood Story—Bree Jones." *Spiritual Capital*. Podcast audio. December 4, 2020. https://open.spotify.com/episode/5vZP5ZgBnKCfXeU KRrLwCt?si=NGEiDe5sTUKioVkjmRZ5Hw.

————. "You Are Not Your Start Up—Allen Woods." *Spiritual Capital*. Podcast audio. October 1, 2020. https://open.spotify.com/episode/6fzvr6kaPW7yA33hypyhUC? si=8aVchUchT5OZPF-RW-zwGg.

McCarraher, Eugene. *The Enchantments of Mammon: How Capitalism Became the Religion of Modernity*. Cambridge: Belknap, 2020.

Meagher, Sean. "A Neighbourhood Vitality Index: An Approach to Measuring Neighbourhood Well-Being." United Way of Greater Toronto.

Miller, David. *God at Work: The History and Promise of the Faith at Work Movement*. New York: Oxford University Press, 2007.

Miller, Donald. *Building a Story Brand*. New York: HarperCollins Publishers, 2017.

Mori, Masahiro. "The Uncanny Valley." *Energy* 7 (1970) 33–35. http://www. androidscience.com/theuncannyvalley/proceedings2005/uncannyvalley.html.

"My B Impact Score Only Increased by a Few Points, but Our Impact Has Increased Dramatically. What Happened?" B Impact Assessment. Accessed December 15, 2020. http://bimpactassessment.net/how-it-works/frequently-asked-questions/ the-b-impact-score#my-b-impact-score-only-increased-by-a-few-points,-but-our-impact-has-increased-dramatically.—what-happened.

Nonko, Emily. "Minneapolis' Somali-American Community Can Soon Bypass the Bank to Buy Homes." *Wisconsin Muslim Journal*. September 3, 2019. https:// wisconsinmuslimjournal.org/minneapolis-somali-american-community-can-soon-bypass-the-bank-to-buy-homes/.

Noor, Poppy. "There are plenty more like Cambridge Analytica. I know—I've used the data." *The Guardian*. March 23, 2018. https://www.theguardian.com/comment isfree/2018/mar/23/plenty-more-like-cambridge-analytica-data-facebook.

Odom, Dave. "How to Nurture a Christian Way of Life." *Faith & Leadership*. January 9, 2018. https://faithandleadership.com/dave-odom-how-nurture-christian-way-life.

Packer, George. "The President Is Winning His War on American Institutions." *The Atlantic*. April 2020. https://www.theatlantic.com/magazine/archive/2020/04/ how-to-destroy-a-government/606793/.

Peters, John Durham. "The Gaps of Which Communication Is Made." *Critical Studies in Mass Communication* 11 (1994) 117–40.

————. *Speaking into the Air: A History of the Idea of Communication*. Chicago: University of Chicago Press, 1999.

Peterson, Anne Helen. *Can't Even: How Millennials Became the Burnout Generation*. Boston: Houghton Mifflin Harcourt, 2020.

———. "How Millennials Became The Burnout Generation." Buzzfeed News. January 5, 2019. Accessed September 28, 2020. https://www.buzzfeednews.com/article/annehelenpetersen/millennials-burnout-generation-debt-work.

Piil, Maiken. "Meet Maiken." Accessed December 16, 2020. https://maikenpiil.com/.

Plato. *Phaedrus*. Translated by Alexander Nehamas and Paul Woodruff. Indianapolis: Hackett, 1995.

Princen, Thomas. *The Logic of Sufficiency*. Cambridge: MIT Press, 2005.

Putnam, Robert. *Bowling Alone: The Collapse and Revival of American Community*. New York: Simon & Schuster, 2000.

Rabb, Chris. *Invisible Capital: How Unseen Forces Shape Entrepreneurial Opportunity*. San Francisco: Berrett-Koehler, 2010.

"The (RED) Manifesto." Internet Archive Wayback Machine. August 19, 2007. http://web.archive.org/web/20071210121154/www.joinred.com/manifesto/.

"The (RED) Manifesto." Modernista! Flickr. January 1, 2007. http://www.flickr.com/photos/modernistaboston/916245353/#/photos/modernistaboston/916245353/lightbox/.

Richards, I. A. *Principles of Literary Criticism*. New York: Routledge & Kegan Paul, 1924.

Rickert, Thomas J. *Ambient Rhetoric: The Attunements of Rhetorical Being*. Pittsburgh: University of Pittsburgh Press, 2013.

"Rooted Good." Rooted Good. Accessed December 20, 2020. https://rootedgood.org/.

Rose, Nikolas. *Governing the Soul: The Shaping of the Private Self*. 2nd ed. London: Free Association, 1999.

Rutte, Martin. *Project Heaven on Earth: The 3 simple questions that will help you change the world . . . easily.* 3 Questions, 2018.

Sampson, Mark. "*The Promise of Social Enterprise: A Theological Exploration of Faithful Economic Practice.*" PhD diss., King's College, 2018.

Seerveld, Cal, trans. "Ecclesiastes." Unpublished manuscript.

"Shannon Hopkins: The gamification of innovation." *Faith & Leadership*. November 1, 2016. https://faithandleadership.com/shannon-hopkins-gamification-innovation.

Sinek, Simon. *Start with Why: How Great Leaders Inspire Everyone to Take Action*. New York: Portfolio/Penguin: 2009.

Taylor, Charles. *A Secular Age*. Cambridge: Belknap, 2007.

Taylor, James R. "Dialogue as the Search for Sustainable Organizational Co-Orientation." In *Dialogue: Theorizing Difference in Communication Studies*, edited by Rob Anderson, et al. Thousand Oaks: SAGE, 2004.

Thompson, Deanna A. *The Virtual Body of Christ in a Suffering World*. Nashville: Abingdon, 2016.

Thompson, Derek. "Workism Is Making Americans Miserable." *The Atlantic*. February 24, 2019. Accessed September 28, 2020. https://www.theatlantic.com/ideas/archive/2019/02/religion-workism-making-americans-miserable/583441/.

Thrift, Nigel. *Knowing Capitalism*. London: SAGE, 2005.

Tippett, Krista. "The Conversational Nature of Reality." On Being. Podcast audio. April 7, 2016. https://onbeing.org/programs/david-whyte-the-conversational-nature-of-reality/.

"The Truth isn't Sexy." Matryoshka Haus. 2007. https://www.matryoshkahaus.com/what-we-do/projects/the-truth-isnt-sexy/.

Verter, Brandon. "Spiritual Capital: Theorizing Religion with Bourdieu Against Bourdieu." *Sociological Theory* 21 (2003) 150–74.

Volf, Miroslav. *Exclusion and Embrace.* Nashville: Abingdon, 1996.

Webb, Stephen. *The Gifting God: A Trinitarian Ethics of Excess.* New York: Oxford University Press, 1996.

Weiss, Carol Hirschon. "Nothing as Practical as Good Theory: Exploring Theory-based Evaluation for Comprehensive Community Initiatives for Children and Families." In *New Approaches to Evaluating Community Initiatives: Concepts, Methods, and Contexts,* edited by James Connell, et al. Washington, DC: Aspen Institute, 1995.

"What Makes the Assessment Different than Other Systems?" B Impact Assessment. Accessed December 15, 2020. http://bimpactassessment.net/how-it-works/frequently-asked-questions/the-basics#what-makes-the-assessment-different-than-other-systems.

White, Robert. "From Giving to Investing: Social Enterprises Change the Philanthropic Paradigm." January 19, 2017. https://redf.org/latest/from-giving-to-investing-social-enterprises-change-the-philanthropic-paradigm-bob-white-cara/.

Whyte, David. *Consolations: The Solace, Nourishment and Underlying Meaning of Everyday Words.* Langley: Many Rivers, 2015.

————. *Pilgrim.* Langley: Many Rivers, 2016.

Wilson, Lindsay. *Job.* Grand Rapids: Eerdmans, 2015.

Woods, Allen. "I'm not okay and I can't find the right words." https://mailchi.mp/wearemortar/im-not-okay-and-i-cant-find-the-right-words?e=fdc96c7abd.

Wuthnow, Robert. *After Heaven: Spirituality in America Since the 1950s.* Berkeley: University of Southern California Press, 1998.

Zohar, Danah, and Ian Marshall. *Spiritual Capital: Wealth We Can Live By.* San Francisco: Berrett-Koehler, 2004.

Subject Index